BASIC ILLUSTRATED
Canoe
Paddling

Harry Roberts
Revised by Steve Salins

Illustrated by Lon Levin

FALCONGUIDES ®

GUILFORD, CONNECTICUT
HELENA, MONTANA
AN IMPRINT OF THE GLOBE PEQUOT PRESS

Text and page design by Karen Williams [intudesign.net]
Photos © istockphoto

Library of Congress Cataloging-in-Publication Data is available.

ISBN 978-0-7627-4758-0

Printed in China
First Edition/First Printing

To buy books in quantity for corporate use
or incentives, call **(800) 962–0973,**
or e-mail **premiums@GlobePequot.com.**

The authors and The Globe Pequot Press assume no liability for accidents happening to, or injuries sustained by, readers who engage in the activities described in this book.

Contents

Acknowledgments

Thanks to Ted Bell, Mike Cichanowski, Dan Cooke, Craig Johnson, Dave Kruger, Jim Mandle, Bill Ostrom, Bear Paulson, Larry Rice, Tony Way, Brian and Sonja Wieber, and Charlie Wilson. Huge accolades also go out to Bell Canoe Works and We-no-nah Canoe for their technical advice on modern canoe design and construction.

Appreciation goes to these companies for use of selected photos: Chota Outdoor Gear, Bell Canoe Works, Dagger Canoe Company, We-no-nah Canoe Company, Larry Ricker/LHR Images.

Foreword

This pleasant little book was originally written in a folksy, direct, energetic style as *Basic Essentials Canoe Paddling* by Harry Roberts. Though I never met him, my familiarity with his many articles and ad copy for Sawyer Canoes, coupled with an appreciation of his style and evangelistic enthusiasm for bent-shaft paddling, brought me, as a beginning paddler, many moments of pleasure and insight. After he died, I felt honored when asked to revise and update this work, and I made every effort not to lose the unique elements that defined Uncle Harry's style as well as his message of efficient and effective canoe paddling using his beloved "North American Touring Technique."

Canoe paddling has been around for centuries, or perhaps millennia. Since the mid-eighteen hundreds, the classic style of using straight-shaft paddles with multiple varied strokes was the foundation of canoe instruction. However, some four to five decades ago, marathon racers (led by the incomparable Gene Jensen) developed and perfected an efficient paddling style using paddles built with an angle between the shaft and blade. Biomechanically, their "sit-n-switch" style required them to sit, not kneel. To conserve energy for long races, they switched sides to steer rather than using classic steering strokes, which "scrub off" forward motion (Harry's phrase, and quite a descriptive one at that). It took a few years for instructors and recreational paddlers to embrace this method of paddling for casual use. However, Uncle Harry was a leading proponent of this style for recreational paddlers, and in his Introduction, he warns the reader to expect instruction that is different from what may have been learned "about paddling in the past."

This paddler, having raced marathons and logged hundreds of recreational miles on flatwater, heartily endorses Uncle Harry's contention that the "sit-an-switch" bent-shaft paddle method is the easiest way to learn to paddle and provides the most efficient technique to move a canoe across a body of water. It's not only simple to understand and easy to learn; it satisfies a beginner's instinct to switch sides when paddling a craft that resists every effort to move in a straight line.

Any temptation to expand this work to include instruction on classical canoeing style is mitigated by a strong commitment to remain true to Harry Roberts's intent and passion. When first published, his book was as simple, direct, and effective an instruction manual for using a bent-shaft paddle as any available. Though it has been twice revised and slightly reorganized to provide clarity and logical progression, the book's original intent and flavor remain unchanged. The reader will notice occasions that identify advantages of using a straight-shaft paddle for some strokes (pry, low brace) as well as for whitewater canoeing. However, for the type of canoeing most of us do—flatwater touring and very easy rivers—Harry Roberts's presentation of bent-shaft paddling technique provides all the necessary tools to effectively control a canoe in most situations.

More important than technical instruction is the passion for canoeing that Uncle Harry weaves with his words. His encouragement to enjoy the inherent pleasures of simply and comfortably moving a canoe through water is refreshing and uplifting. His "Take-Out" comments at the end of the book remain unchanged from the original work. Read them first; he captures the emotion, passion, and feelings of the most committed of us. There may be no finer tribute to paddling ever written.

Steve Salins
Seattle
January 2006

Introduction

This book is about paddling. It's not about selecting a canoe. It's not about tents or sleeping bags or cooking gear or portage packs. It's about paddling. Because paddling is, in my experience, the part of canoeing that's frequently forgotten, even though it's the part of canoeing that can make or break your trip.

There's a popular notion that anybody can paddle. Let's rephrase that. Anybody can be taught to paddle. Paddle well, paddle easily, paddle efficiently, paddle in control, and paddle safely.

But why bother, you ask? Millions of people go canoeing every weekend and seem to be having a good time, and most of them don't paddle well. Why bother?

Well, are you sure they're having a good time? If they were, they'd be out on the water next week, maybe even the next day, in their own canoe. The fact is that most have a good time swimming, or fishing, or splashing water and tipping over, or (in what's come to be a noxious tradition on many waterways) getting drunk and rowdy. A few enjoy watching birds, sensing the constant variations of light dancing on the water, and slipping into a oneness with the natural world. But very few enjoy paddling for its own merits. Very few get involved in the feel of a canoe slipping quickly, easily, and powerfully through the water under perfect and nearly unconscious control. Very few paddle well enough to be free to absorb the world around them without worrying about wind, waves, current, or even fundamentals like keeping the boat going straight.

In simple terms, learning to paddle well gives you the skills to enjoy canoeing more. Who knows? You might even find yourself catching an hour on the water every day after dinner! Most of us live close enough to a paddleable waterway to do just that. But you'll never do that unless you enjoy paddling— the art and craft of making a canoe do exactly what you want it to do when you want it to.

So, we'll be talking together about the easiest way to learn to paddle. And I mean easiest. This isn't the School of One Thousand Strokes

And a Stroke! It's a couple of strokes—but strokes learned so well that you don't have to think about them. And before we start, I'd like to ask you one favor. This is a contemporary approach to paddling. If you've learned a bit about paddling in the past, as I did, you'll be confused by some of what you'll read. You'll be told that it's not only okay to sit in a canoe, but that it's generally preferable. You probably won't recognize the paddle I'll recommend. And you'll be told that switching sides when you paddle is a sign of artistry, not of terminal ineptitude.

This is a new way to paddle, at least new to a lot of folks. Its fancy name is "North American Touring Technique," and I confess I coined that name for it. Marathon racers—those men and women who paddle long distances in skinny canoes at average speeds of over seven miles per hour on dead flat water—call it "sit-and-switch." It's an accurate name. You do sit in the canoe, and you do switch paddling sides to aid in directional control, to encourage more efficient strokes, and to distribute the effort to powerful muscle groups. But "sit-and-switch" is an unlovely phrase at best, evoking memories of parental discipline rather than thoughts of clear water and the sound of a canoe running at speed. Clearly, the name needed some gussying up. So, it became North American Touring Technique, or NATT for short.

The name's a mouthful. And I promise I won't use it again until the last chapter in the book. But when you start paddling this way, and you just plain flat-out blow the rails off your companions and get to the takeout so far ahead of them that you're able to read the first half of Anna Karenina and still add three birds to your life list, I'd appreciate it if you'd tell your friends the full name for the way you paddle. It'd make me feel good. It really would.

And it'd make me feel good to see the looks of astonishment on the faces of your paddling buddies when you and your partner just take off and leave them, with smiles on your faces and a notable absence of sweat on your brows. I won't be there, of course. But I've seen that look enough to know what it is, and I'm smiling already.

I've run off at the mouth enough. Zip up your PFD and let's go paddling!

CHAPTER 1

Starting Right

I can only assume you already have a canoe and a partner who's willing to forgive you your trespasses. If you don't, I'd need a book of about this size to talk about the process of selecting a canoe. Yeah, there are that many choices, and design differences can be subtle. But, since we don't have that other book, I'll have to assume that you own a canoe and that your primary intent is to take that canoe somewhere and look at something. If you lust for the thrill of playing in whitewater, you've bought the wrong book. If you drool over sea kayaks, you've bought the wrong book. What can I tell you?

Your Paddle

When it's time to go somewhere in a canoe, the paddle that maintains both nice control and efficient paddling is a "bent-shaft" paddle: one in which the blade angles away from the shaft at approximately fifteen degrees. I can hear you now: "Buy another paddle?" Yup, that's right. When you're ready to move a canoe, there is no more efficient tool for making it happen than a bent-shaft paddle. What we're talking about here is movement, glide, power, efficiency, cruisin'—that which makes paddling fun and draws you out on the water again and again!

Your outfitter should know what you mean when you tell him you want a fifteen-degree bent shaft, although when you

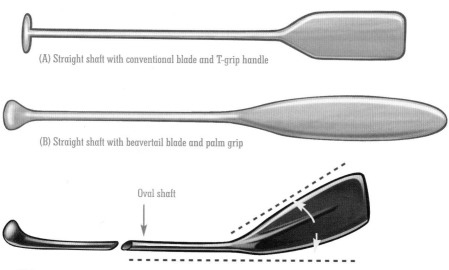

(A) Straight shaft with conventional blade and T-grip handle

(B) Straight shaft with beavertail blade and palm grip

Oval shaft

(C) Bent shaft with conventional blade and palm grip

FIGURE 1–1:

Straight- and bent-shaft paddles.

see one, you may think it's damaged, because there will be an angle between the shaft and blade.

You probably already have some paddles. If you bought your canoe from a shop, the salesperson may have added or sold you some inexpensive paddles. If you got a "pre-paddled" canoe, the previous owner may have included old paddles as incentive for you to pay his asking price. In any case, you more than likely have a couple straight paddling sticks to get you started. That's okay; keep them. As we go along, we will point out when using a "straight shaft" paddle is more effective. If you plan to paddle your canoe on a whitewater river, a straight-shaft paddle gives you more control for whitewater moves. Meanwhile, for flatwater lakes, ponds, bogs, and easy rivers, the bent-shaft paddle I recommend will allow you to paddle more easily and efficiently.

Why a bent shaft of about fifteen degrees? Simple. A paddle functions efficiently within a range of fifteen degrees to either side of vertical. Build in the angle to begin with, and you can use a shorter, less tiring stroke with a shorter, lighter, handier paddle. Who wouldn't buy that? I recommend a blade width of no more than 8 inches and a blade length of 18 to 20 inches. Why? A moderately small blade won't twist in your hand under power, and it will be less tiring to paddle. Some paddle makers shave the shoulders of the blade to make a teardrop shape. With less surface area, the blade is plenty effective, less tiring, and in the water can better tuck alongside the canoe.

I insist the shaft be oval rather than round so it fits more comfortably in my lower hand. Furthermore, an oval shaft helps me control exactly how my blade enters the water. I also want the grip—that knob on the top of the shaft—to be what's generally called a "palm grip." Paddling correctly, you push down on the paddle shaft, and a palm grip is more comfortable in the upper hand for that action.

Now, how do you fit this unusual paddle? Size is important here;

FIGURE 1–2:

Sizing a bent-shaft paddle to determine base shaft length.

Nose level

Base shaft length

you'd make sure hiking boots fit perfectly, and your paddle should fit you no less well. When you go to your outfitter, have him sit you on a flat chair or bench. Turn the paddle upside down, and place the handle on the bench between your legs with the shaft vertical. If you're sitting erect, your nose should touch the throat of the paddle, that place on the paddle where blade changes to shaft. That measurement, from bench to nose, is called base shaft length. I don't know what canoe you're paddling, but unless it's a big tripping boat with a flared bow, a bent-shaft paddle with a shaft length of that measurement will do you nicely. If you paddle a big tripper, one that's 25 inches wide or more from rail to rail at the bow seat, consider a paddle with a shaft length an inch or two longer.

If, in spite of my open, honest manner and reputation for trustworthiness, you prefer a straight-shaft paddle because some guru told you to use one for better canoe control, add 6 to 8 inches to that base shaft length. (Maybe you better bring those paddles you got with the canoe along with you to the outfitter, just in case you need to check the length!)

Okay. I brought up the subject of control, so I'd best deal with it right now. If you're paddling whitewater—and that doesn't mean "running a rapid," it means "playing" a rapid—I'm quick to concede the control strokes you'll use are better done with a straight-shaft paddle. So keep the straight-shaft paddles you may have and we'll talk about those strokes later. If, however, you're a "going somewhere" paddler, you can make a canoe do anything you need it to do with a bent-shaft paddle. And for probably 90 percent of your paddling, you can do it as well and more efficiently. If you couldn't, the folks who paddle marathon canoe races and the folks who race open canoes downriver in whitewater would be using straight-shaft paddles. They don't.

So much for the paddle . . . almost. If you're buying paddles, may I suggest that a degree of equivalency be maintained between what the bow paddler gets and what the stern paddler gets. I've been in this game a long time, and all too often I've seen The Captain of the Ship buy himself the latest and lightest, and get the First Mate (otherwise known as "wife," because no girlfriend would put up with such

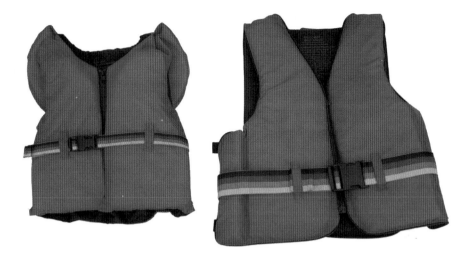

A Personal Flotation Device (PFD) for a child and adult.

nonsense) a heavy, clumsy club that he wouldn't use as a spare, because it's "good enough." Get paddles that feel good and look good, and you'll enjoy them more.

Your Life Jacket (PFD)

Every state mandates that you have a U.S. Coast Guard–approved PFD (Personal Flotation Device) on board for each passenger. When I'm teaching, I require each paddler in my class to wear a PFD, and I wear one myself. Learn to paddle while wearing a PFD, and you won't feel uncomfortable with one on. Yeah, I know. Paddling's a barefoot sport, a sun-and-sand sport, and a PFD sort of spoils the image. So does drowning. Wear the PFD. Sure, there'll be times in nonthreatening warm water on a warm day when you can slip out of the PFD. That's a judgment call. But you're just learning to paddle. You're just learning which situations are threatening and which are not. Until you know, wear the PFD all the time. If you're less than confident as a swimmer, wear the PFD all the time. It's a confidence-builder and a warm, cozy buddy when the chilly winds pick up.

What kind to get? The kind your canoe shop might call a "paddling vest." It looks like a vest made of closed-cell foam strips or soft foam covered with nylon. It has a zipper closure and a waist belt that either ties or buckles. It should fit you comfortably. Too tight is, well, too tight, and too loose means that it could ride up over your head when you least want it to. It shouldn't bite your neck, and it shouldn't bind under your arms. Your canoe shop can advise you on the fine points of it. Try it on, and paddle the air. If it chafes in the shop, it will chafe on the water. Get one that feels comfortable all around.

A good PFD will set you back $60 to $120. If that seems like a lot, consider that if it fits well, looks good, and is comfortable, you'll wear it. And if you wear it, it will do you some good when you need it. You can get cheap orange horse- collar PFDs or flotation cushions for much less. Either will fulfill your obligation under most boating laws. So why not get them? The horse collar fits so badly that you won't wear it, and it's of dubious value as a protective device because it leaves your back unprotected. The flotation cushion is great for a lunch break, but do you really think you're going to be able to get to it if your boat overturns, or if you take a nose-dive out of your boat and wind or current carries your boat and cushion away? Get a good PFD. Wear it. End of sermon.

Outfitting Your Canoe

If you're not comfortable in a canoe, you won't paddle it much. And if you're not part of your canoe, you won't paddle it well—or easily. Fortunately, the tweaking you do for comfort is the same tweaking to fit you solidly in the canoe for good control and efficiency. The key is to have your seat, knees, and feet locked firmly in the canoe. Let's get to it!

First a little theory. When you plant the paddle in the water and pull, you're pulling yourself and the canoe to the paddle (and past it, because the canoe keeps moving after your stroke). If you're snug in your canoe, this works well. If you're not, then you slide around in the canoe. You lose power, efficiency, control, and if the truth be known, you aren't comfortable. Wasted effort and discomfort doesn't beckon you to go paddling again.

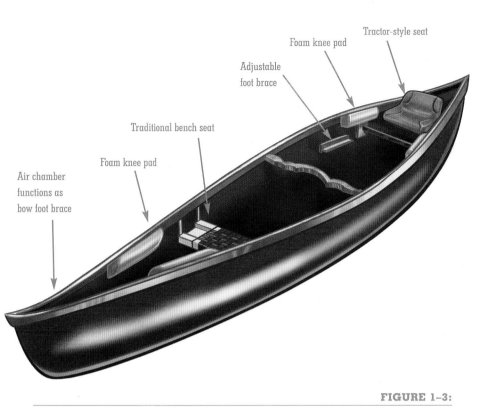

Tractor-style seat

Foam knee pad

Adjustable
foot brace

Traditional bench seat

Foam knee pad

Air chamber
functions as
bow foot brace

FIGURE 1–3:

Outfitting your canoe with seats, foot braces, and knee pads.

Comfort starts with the seat. Your canoe will have either some sort of bench-style seat (generally a flat frame supporting a caned insert or nylon webbing) or a tractor-style bucket seat (which looks just like its name). The wonderful thing about a tractor-style seat is that it holds your backside firmly in place, giving you something to push against as well as preventing you from sliding around. If you have a bench seat, you can tape or glue foam pieces to the seat to accomplish a similarly firm fit.

Either type of seat can be padded with thin, closed-cell foam of the sort backpackers carry. Some folks opt to enclose the foam in a comfy fabric. I suppose there's merit in that, but not in the damp maritime climate I live with on the shores of Lake Huron. If the seat pad were detachable, you could convince me. Perhaps hold the pad in place with Velcro? Remember, there will be hot, muggy days when you want air ventilating around your seat, so leave yourself the option to remove the pad. Also, remember to provide a seat drain for the water on rainy days.

It's worthwhile having a seat that supports your backside. That's so you can push against it while it holds you in place as you paddle. Your feet should be braced against a solid object. That could be gear, a dowel rod anchored to the seat by a cord, or a telescoping foot brace that can be adjusted for leg length. You may not always have gear when you paddle, and a dowel rod set-up isn't solid, plus the cord could tangle your feet in a capsize. The best choice for the stern paddler is to install a firm, adjustable foot brace. If your local paddling shop doesn't carry foot braces, you can order them from a manufacturer who produces fast, efficient flatwater canoes. For a bow paddler, the end wall of the flotation chamber is often used as a foot brace. If you paddle a canoe that doesn't have end flotation chambers, it may be worthwhile to carve a foam block to fit; not only will you add flotation, but also a solid foot brace for the bow paddler.

Now don't forget your knees. Manufacturers design gunwales to be strong and attractive, but you want to lock your knees against the inside of that gunwale and sometimes it's a sharp edge punctuated by rivets. Ideally, your thighs should be parallel to the gunwale so you don't have to reach out to paddle over bent knees. For more comfort and better control, glue some foam along the inside gunwale of your canoe where your knees and thighs lock in.

We've been assuming you're sitting in your canoe and that's because we're talking about an efficient paddling technique with bent-shaft paddles. But the high priests of this game aren't so rigid as to disallow kneeling. If you're going to be a kneeler using a straight-shaft paddle, then you still need solid points of contact with your canoe. Start with a set of foam knee pads on the bottom of the canoe. They not only soften your knee position, but also keep your knees from sliding around inside the canoe. Glue the pads in place, set comfortably apart in the chines of the canoe (where the bottom meets the side). Whitewater paddlers install thigh straps to keep their knees solidly connected to the boat, and I've known a flatwater paddler or two who uses thigh straps for the same reason.

If your seat is placed so low that you bump your armpits against the rails, raise the seat. If the seat is so high that you feel uncomfortable in the canoe, lower the seat.

If the canoe doesn't ride level in the water with you and your partner in it, move the bow seat forward or aft to give your canoe a nearly level trim. Move the stern seat, too, if you must. Be sure your canoe is always trimmed slightly stern-heavy. (To check your trim, pour a bailer full of water into the canoe. The water should gravitate toward the stern.) If you want to get fancy—or just plain do the job right to begin with—mount a sliding seat in the bow. If that doesn't give you a level trim, mount a stern slider as well. If there's a substantial weight discrepancy between you and your partner, go directly to the bow and stern slider setup, or rig the canoe to allow mounting an extra set of seats placed in such a way as to permit you to switch places.

Switch places? Isn't that heresy? Maybe for some, but if you paddle with the bent-shaft style I recommend, you should be able to paddle bow or stern with anybody else who paddles this style. You'll be able to paddle from either side with aplomb. And if you're used to being the Captain sitting in the stern and barking orders to the Mate, you're in for a rude awakening. A pleasant awakening, actually. It's easy to flip a bass bug at a log when you're in the bow. (Darn! Don't let Molly read this, or I'll be back in the stern again!)

Anyway, set the boat up so you can trim it level without gear, so you can keep your butt fixed in place when you're working, and so you have somewhere to plant your feet. If you can do all that yourself, fine. If you can't, go to your friendly local canoe dealer and solicit his help. While you're there, you might ask him why in hell he didn't sell you a boat with a bow slider and foot braces in the first place!

Getting Into Your Canoe

Oops! Forgot something. Would you believe that getting into and out of a canoe is when most upsets occur? Yep. It's true. Take it to the bank. And believe me, nothing can squelch the joy of a day on the water like a thorough soaking before you even get in the boat.

Canoes are stable craft. It's paddlers that make canoes unstable. Set a canoe adrift in whitewater or on a big lake when the whitecaps are rolling, and the canoe will take care of itself. Add two paddlers, and you raise the center of gravity and roll center of the canoe, and the canoe loses some of its rock-solid stability. A modicum of common sense and a pinch of learning will compensate for that once you're on the water. But going from the bank to the water is tricky. A canoe isn't very stable when its bow is on shore, its stern balanced precariously on the river bottom, and nothing but air under its middle. It also isn't very strong. Canoes are designed to be strong when supported by water, not when supported precariously on both ends. More canoes are tipped over and damaged by paddlers getting in and getting out than are damaged even on whitewater streams.

I don't want to talk this point to death. This isn't exactly a spiritual crisis we're dealing with, after all. There are many ways to enter and move around in a canoe, depending on circumstances, but all of them depend on two things. One is keeping your weight-bearing foot on the center line of the canoe, and the other is balancing the canoe side-to-side by transferring some of your weight to your hands, each placed on a gunwale of the canoe.

Here's one way to get the job done. Put the entire boat in the water parallel to the shore in water a few inches deep. While you're learning, put your paddles in the canoe where (1) you can reach them easily, and (2) you won't trip over them. (Later on, after you've done this a few times, you'll keep hold of your paddle with one hand while you get in and out because a good canoeist always hangs on to his paddle!) Both paddlers grasp both gunwales (rails) of the canoe to keep it steady. You can face each other, or both face forward. One of you, often the stern partner, gets in first.

Canoes are designed to be strong when supported by water. Most canoes are tipped over and damaged by paddlers getting in and getting out than are damaged on whitewater streams.

Now do like I already told you: Keep your body bent over to keep your center of gravity as low as possible, and step into the canoe, placing your foot right smack in the middle of the canoe right over the keel line. Balancing your weight on both hands and your foot, swing yourself in and kneel or sit down on the seat. One more time now: hands on both rails, body low, knees flexed, first foot dead in the center of the boat. Once you're in and settled, your partner will get in the same way. While he's doing that, you might want to lean the canoe a little bit to the side and put your paddle on the bottom like a pole to stabilize the canoe while he gets in.

When you're both seated comfortably, pick up your paddles. Your feet may be wet, but that's no big deal. The rest of you is dry, and the boat is floating freely, awaiting your further command.

Now that you know how to get in and out, develop a feel for good balance. Place a foot in the center of the canoe and stand in a crouched-over position with your hands on the gunwales, sort of like a sprinter ready to come out of starting blocks. Put some weight on your hands and rock the boat back and forth. Feel pretty comfortable? Can you wave your other foot in the air behind you without feeling nervous? Good; if you keep your weight centered, low, and balanced, your canoe will take care of you, and that's a good thing to learn.

Now there are fancy sculling maneuvers that you can use to move the boat into water deep enough for paddling. And these maneuvers look sharp and make you feel good about yourself. Someday we'll talk about sculling, but it will be at another time and place. For now, gently push yourself away with the paddles. I promise I won't tell anybody that you did it that way if you won't tell anybody that I told you to do it.

The Basic Forward Stroke

Over ninety-five percent of your paddle strokes will be made to move your canoe in a straight line, and ninety-five percent of the rest of your strokes will be simple control and turning strokes that are little more than a forward stroke taken in a different direction other than parallel to the keel line of your canoe. It's clear that mastering an effective forward stroke lays a solid foundation for virtually all of your paddling.

Now before we make a mad dash to the water with canoe and life jackets, let's be sure to hold the paddle properly and understand which side of the blade is the power face. The power face is the side that pulls the canoe through the water in a forward stroke. If you have a bent-shaft paddle, as I suggest, you're going to have to figure out which is the power face. But that's easy; when the paddle shaft is vertical, the blade should angle forward (Figure 2-1). If you need another clue, you can usually tell by the comfort of the grip; most bent-shaft paddles have a hand grip that feels comfortable one way and not the other. If you have a straight-shaft paddle, either side can be the power face. Pick a side and stick a piece of tape on it so you can keep track of which side you're using as the power face. Done that? Great! Now let's get on the water and get to it.

In the last chapter you were on the water, floating free, with enough depth under the hull that you wouldn't bash your

Torso rotated, shoulder forward

Hand high, ready to push down

Arm forward

FIGURE 2-1:

Paddling position, ready to go.

paddle on the bottom. Now before we go anywhere, I have to tell you Robert's Rule #1: "Two shall not paddle on the same side of the canoe, lest the sea rise up and bite them in the butt." So you're going to have to agree who paddles on which side. It won't matter for long, because using bent-shaft paddles, you're going to switch sides (together) anyway. If you're using straight-shaft paddles, steering strokes come from the stern paddler, and paddlers don't switch sides unless they're tired. It makes sense for the stern to paddle on his or her most comfortable side. So let the stern paddler choose, and the bow will paddle the other side.

While we're at it, I may as well tell you Robert's Rule #2: "Two shall paddle together, in sync, harmoniously, simultaneously, lest the canoe rise up and dump them in the drink." How do you do that? It's easy: The stern paddler watches the bow paddler and exactly matches his or her stroke rate. So let's sum up. You and your partner paddle on opposite sides and you paddle together. That's not so hard to remember, is it? Good. Now you won't look like rookies on the water.

Making the Canoe Go

Okay, now hold the palm grip—that funny little knob on the top of the paddle shaft—with one hand. That's your "upper" hand. With your other hand (the "lower" hand), grasp the paddle shaft about two to three hand-widths above the "throat," the point where the shaft becomes the blade. The throat is also the location of the "bend" on a bent-shaft paddle. Avoid a death grip on your paddle. Hold it with the same tenderness as you'd hold a baby. You want to learn to paddle relaxed and loose.

Now, sit erect but "easy," like a big league shortstop waiting on the pitcher to throw the ball. To begin the stroke, rotate your upper body a little, leading with the shoulder on your paddling side. Place the paddle in the water, with the blade vertical, or nearly so, and your arms nearly straight and away from your body. It's important that your upper hand reaches high across your body and is out over the water so your paddle is vertical. To move the canoe, push down with your upper hand as you rotate your torso to pull the paddle blade back with your lower hand.

FIGURE 2–2:

Paddling opposite sides in perfect sync.

Body and shoulder rotation

Upper hand high and over the water, pushes down on shaft

Lower arm pulls back with body rotation

Blade movement

Bent-shaft blade angles forward when shaft is vertical

FIGURE 2–3:

Forward stroke.

As you finish your stroke, let the paddle slide out of the water and, using the same rotation, place the paddle back into the water, again pulling yourself up to the paddle by "unwinding" your upper body . . . and so on. It's a simple repetitive move that, in a sense, keeps the shoulder of your top hand almost still and the rest of your upper body rotating around it. The key here is a body twist (rotation) that brings major muscles of the back into play.

Okay? Erect but not stiff? Rotating your upper body around the fixed point of your "off-side" shoulder? Rotating back to neutral and lifting the paddle out of the water? Paddle blade vertical, or nearly so? Good. Even if it doesn't feel normal, it's a good start. With time and practice it will feel natural.

Your arms really don't do much in a good touring stroke. It's not strictly correct to say they do nothing, but the real engines that drive the boat are the large muscles of your back, shoulders, and belly. And they can drive the boat easily because your feet are planted, your backside isn't slipping, and you have a firm foundation against which to work.

Some practice exercises will help you get the feel of paddling correctly. For a few strokes, lock your elbows so your arms are straight and rigid. Now paddle. Yep, it feels awkward, but it makes the boat go. Do you feel your back working? Do you notice how you have to rotate to make it work? Good. That's the feeling you should have in your back all the time when you're pulling your canoe through the water, even with your elbows unlocked.

Focus on your upper hand. Pretend it's a piston that simply moves up and down. Your hand rises high, pushes down on the paddle shaft, then rises straight back up to prepare for the next stroke. Make it go straight up and down. You'll find your stroke will be much more vertical, you'll feel the power of your downstroke shifting to the angled blade in the water, and you'll notice your lower hand sliding out to the side just enough to clear the blade above the water on the recovery part of your stroke.

When you combine the piston action of your upper hand with your body rotation, you pull with your back, and you're on your way to developing an efficient, powerful forward stroke. You don't always have to paddle with dramatic action, but your paddling engine will be idling along and can be revved up as needed to handle wind, current, or a race.

Now here's the tricky bit. You've paddled a few strokes, and the boat is starting to move along. But it's turning away from the paddling side of the stern paddler. And it may be bobbing and diving and feeling wiggly. Let the boat glide nearly to a stop and start over again. Bow paddler: Do that simple, repetitive stroke in a regular, metronome-like rhythm. It needn't be fast; that comes with practice. One stroke every two seconds is just fine for starters. Remember, you're learning a habit pattern, and you want to get it right. Stern paddler, match your partner's tempo. Place your paddle in the water at the same time, rotate your upper body through the same degree of arc, slide your paddle out of the water at the same time, and so forth. Just like dancing together.

Going Straight

By now the old canoe should be running along pretty nicely, but it still wants to turn away from the stern paddler's side. Don't worry; that's normal. But we're going to fix it. If you look at a canoe with two paddlers in it, the stern paddler's paddle is farther away from the centerline of the canoe, and his or her stroke is also nearer to the canoe's center of rotation than the bow paddler's stroke. Physical law dictates the canoe has to turn away from the stern's stroke. (Sorry, stern buddy; you're not "overpowering" your partner. Unflex those biceps, spit out your chew of Red Man, reduce the testosterone, and unclench!) The canoe will continue to turn unless you do something to stop it from turning.

Now back at good old Camp Yukintipovurtu, in the days of your youth, you learned something called a J-stroke from a camp counselor who was bored silly, preoccupied with dreams about somebody in a red swimsuit at the camp across the lake, and didn't know much about canoeing to begin with. And the old J-stroke worked, after a fashion. You had a gut feeling that it scrubbed off a lot of the canoe's speed, and was sort of like accelerating away from a stoplight while stabbing the brakes at the same time, but it got you there. Well, your gut was right,

Because the stern paddle is nearer to the canoe's center of rotation than the bow paddle, canoes have a tendency to turn away from the stern paddler's side, thus causing the canoe to not go straight.

and although there is a place for a J-stroke, we won't be using it right now. You'll be doing something else. This is where bent-shaft paddling technique gives you a terrific advantage over the folks using straight paddles.

Think about this. If a bow paddler is paddling on the left and the stern on the right, and the canoe wants to turn left after eight or ten strokes, what's the easiest way to stop it from turning? Right you are: switch sides! In fact, that's what novices do when they first get in a canoe and realize it's not going straight. But if you watch, there is no rhythm to their switches, and the canoe is usually out of control, wildly careening from one side to the other like a drunken sailor. Still, the switching sides theory works; after all, that's how racers paddle long distances at hellishly high speeds. But unlike a novice, we're going to switch with rhythm and a pattern to keep our canoe under control.

When to Switch Sides

Most contemporary canoes are designed to hold a reasonably straight course with little effort because these canoes are designed for touring, and a canoe that requires constant attention to hold a course isn't a pleasant boat for touring. In technical terms, touring canoes are shaped to provide lateral resistance at their stems. It takes a nudge— and in some cases more than that—to overcome that lateral resistance. Once the canoe is up and running, it'll go maybe ten strokes before it begins to turn significantly. One of the more subtle tasks of paddling is to anticipate that inevitable turn to the bow paddler's side and when to switch together, on command, before the canoe is off course and out of control. While you're learning, try switching every six to eight strokes. Adjust as needed to hold your course.

The stern paddler calls the switch, not because he or she is the boss, but for better reasons. A stern paddler can better see and more quickly notice the canoe slipping off course. The stern paddler also can see whether or not the bow paddler has heard the command and switched sides. The bow paddler doesn't have either benefit.

Timing counts for something here. Stern paddler, call the switch at the start of a stroke. This gives your partner time to exit the autopilot mode and react to your call, switching sides at the completion of the stroke. Stern, keep your call a simple monosyllable. "Hut!" is the almost universal call the racers use. It's short, audible, can be grunted, and in legendary racer and designer Gene Jensen's immortal phrase, "You can say it when you're about ready to throw up." Yes, it does sound silly when you first start doing it. It may even sound intrusive in a setting where quiet is called for, although you will learn to adjust your volume to the situation. When it's quiet, a barely audible call works fine; when paddling in a wind, you may have to sing it out because your bow partner may not hear your call. In any case the silly feeling passes quickly. You'll find after fifteen minutes that you can maintain a normal conversation and still say "Hut!" when you need. You (Hut!) won't even hear yourself saying it (Hut!) after a while, and even if your (Hut!) friends think it's nonsense (Hut!), I guarantee that (Hut!) you'll get to the takeout (Hut!) before they do (Hut!) and have first dibs (Hut!) on the cold beer (Hut!) and cheese and French bread (Hut!) you stashed in the car.

Now some folks figure that if you're going to switch sides, you might as well do it automatically on a regular count, like every six strokes. Canoe designer David Yost calls it "The Idiot Six": six power strokes and a switch. It works to maintain direction, but it's a shortcut to mediocrity. For one thing, paddling is supposed to be fun (remember?), and counting "1-2-3-4-5-6-switch, 1-2-3-4. . . ." as you paddle isn't the kind of fun we're talking about here. Besides, there are times when you switch in response to wind, for a change in direction, and for turns. More on that later. For now, become proficient at switching on command and the rest will work out better.

How to Switch Sides

At the completion of the forward stroke, start to remove the paddle from the water and recover as usual. But instead of lifting your top hand for the upward cycle of the "piston" stroke, release your top hand from the grip of the paddle. Meanwhile your lower hand (on the shaft) is going to pass the paddle across your body to your "new" lower

Lower hand passes off
to "new" lower hand

FIGURE 2–4:

Switching sides.

hand, the one you just released (see Figure 2-4). It's not unlike a runner passing a baton in a relay race, except you're going to pass the paddle to yourself. It's best if the new lower hand grabs the paddle shaft under the passing hand. Make the exchange well out in front of your body. As your new lower hand takes control of the paddle shaft, slide your other hand up the shaft to find the grip as you place the paddle in the water for the first stroke on the other side.

    You can practice this sitting on an armless chair. It takes a few minutes of feeling clumsy, but it's easy to learn. If you really want to feel silly, go outside with your partner and your paddles, stand (or sit) in bow/stern alignment, and paddle the air, with the stern calling the switches. Sounds dumb. Looks dumb. Works like a charm. It gets you into a "team" mode very quickly. The bow must react to the stern's call, and the stern must respond to the bow's tempo. Dancin', baby! Dancin'!

Now that you know how to switch to maintain direction efficiently without scrubbing off speed with exaggerated correction strokes, you'll be pleased to know that maintaining speed and direction isn't the only reason for switching sides; it's just one of the reasons. The others? Switching sides lets you equalize the work load on your joints, tendons, and muscles; it enables you to execute powerful, stable turning strokes; and it gives you a real edge in windy conditions.

Review

I prefer to think of the forward stroke as the "power stroke" because you use it to provide power in all directions. It's a little tricky to get right, so let's break it down again and add a few subtleties while we're at it.

Sit erect but not stiff. You should be attached to your canoe with three body points: feet on a foot brace, knees braced on the inside of the gunwale, and backside set solidly in the seat. Keep your legs out in front of you on the foot brace, but not stiff. Thighs should be parallel to and braced against the gunwale; I don't want your bony knees sticking up in the air because they get in the way of a good efficient stroke. When it's time to "lock" yourself in the boat, flex your feet against the foot brace so your knees will better grip the gunwale (you did install some foam, right?) and your butt will be pressed firmly in the tractor-style seat. As you tighten yourself in the canoe, you will be able to control the canoe with your hips.

Hold your paddle loosely, with your arms extended but not stiff. Your forward stroke should be executed comfortably out in front of your body. If you are paddling close to your body, there is no room for power and efficiency, and your switching action will be difficult.

The power of your stroke comes from engaging large muscle

Your forward stroke should be executed comfortably out in front of your body. Paddlers who don't lose power and efficiency and have difficulty executing their switching action.

groups in your back and shoulders. As you progress, you'll become increasingly aware of starting the stroke from your instep, and you'll feel the power flow from the soles of your feet, through your legs, up your rotating torso, and along your arms to the paddle. In fact, you'll begin to notice your leg flex with each pull, and your arms will become simply a "connector" to the paddle to transfer power generated by your rotating torso. To put power into the paddle blade, rotate your upper body around the point of the shoulder of your upper hand. That's the pivot point, not your waist.

Your arms work together as one unit. You don't push with your upper hand and pull with your lower hand. Neither do you cock your lower arm for a little extra snap on the stroke; the power comes from the back and shoulders. Think of your latissimus dorsi muscles as the source of your power. Feel it? Your arms and hands rise and fall; the proper motion is almost up and down, like a piston, rather than forward and back.

As you improve your forward stroke, you'll feel your abdominal muscles tighten up a bit with each stroke. When you really want to make time, you'll straighten up almost imperceptibly as you recover, relax your gut to let a little air sneak in, and tighten down hard in a very brief isometric contraction as you apply power.

You'll notice words like "brief" and "a little" sneaking into this explanation. Here's why. If the tip of your paddle blade travels more than 5 to 7 inches at the point of maximum power, your forward stroke is too long. Remember that maximum power is developed when the paddle blade is within fifteen degrees of either side of vertical. Anything more disturbs the progress of the boat. The bend in your paddle takes care of the forward fifteen degrees and your slight torso rotation and pushing down with your upper hand takes care of the back fifteen degrees. You don't need much rotation; it should be quick, and your paddle should slice from the water as your shoulders come back to square.

Think of the forward stroke in terms of turning a merry-go-round on a playground. Once you get the merry-go-round moving, all it takes is a quick little push on each bar to sustain the movement: quick, frequent, and easy. The idea is to push again on the merry-go-round before it slows. Same with a canoe: once moving, all it takes are quick pushes against the water to keep it moving—quick, frequent, and easy. That's what your paddling should feel like—flick . . . flick . . . flick . . . and the canoe moves smartly along.

Okay, okay. I hear you! You're not a racer. Neither am I anymore. So just slow the stroke down a little to where it's more comfortable, and don't "uncoil" as hard, that's all. Keep the stroke light and easy, but continue to use your whole body. Don't paddle sloppily when you're not in a hurry. In fact, greasing through a backwater to sneak up on a raft of Canada geese is the time to learn to paddle with subtle power and elegance. (And also the time to learn to say "Hut" quietly.)

There's hardly any movement with this stroke. You're still; you're centered over your butt. You're not lunging forward with each stroke to "get more power" because you can't get more power by lunging forward and "punching" your upper hand out. You get the power from your rotation and your drive against the paddle grip, but it's a downward drive, and happens only when the blade has been "set" in the water. Use your head as a paddling style checkpoint: It should not move forward, back, or side-to-side as you paddle.

Some paddlers pull so hard that the bow of the canoe rises and falls. That's called porpoising. Usually the paddler is also lunging and straining. That's no good; it wastes energy. You want to go forward, not up and down. Watch a good paddling team: Some unseen hand pushes the canoe along with no apparent effort. Maintain erect posture and a good stroke technique. Pay attention to your bow; it should move along smartly with nary a hint of up-and-down motion.

Is your paddle exchange smooth, even, and efficient? Go slowly at first so you won't rush the switch. Focus on fully completing each stroke before making the exchange. Shortening up the last stroke because you're in a hurry to switch costs you pulling power and efficiency. Similarly, you should work on getting a full, strong first stroke after every exchange. For practice, agree with your partner to switch on every stroke without command. Go slowly. Make the switches and strokes in a metronomic cadence. As you become proficient, slowly increase your paddling cadence until you are able to make an exchange at speed without missing a beat.

Taking the Paddle Out of the Water

To take the paddle out of the water (the techy term is "recover"), use the same motion in reverse that you did to put the paddle in the water. Up and down, not forward and back. As your upper hand lifts, you'll find your lower hand will have to swing outward just enough so the paddle blade exits and clears the water on its return to the beginning of the next stroke. This motion, called a high recovery, requires minimal motion and is thus the quickest and most efficient way to remove a paddle. Occasionally, when you're bucking the wind, taking your time, or trying to look elegantly stylish, you may want to use a low recovery. Let both hands drop toward your lap and wind up your body as you swing a horizontal paddle across your lap. When you do, you'll have to quickly raise your upper hand at the end of the recovery in order to properly plant the paddle for the next stroke.

While you're paddling, occasionally check your technique. Is your upper hand high and over the water with your paddle shaft vertical? Is your lower hand consistently above or at gunwale level as you paddle? Is your head still, not bobbing around from side to side or lunging forward? Is your paddle shaft vertical as you pull your forward stroke? And is the paddle blade face perpendicular to the direction you are pulling? Good! You've got it figured out. Feels good, doesn't it?

Turning and Correction Strokes

For all my talk about the basic forward stroke, it is only one of the tools in your canoeing tool kit. It's the basic tool, no doubt. But you can't build a cathedral with just one tool. So let's open the tool box, poke around inside, and see what we find. We'll first identify some strokes; in the next chapter we'll tell you how to use them to control your canoe.

When I'm teaching a class on the water, I hardly ever give a name to a stroke or series of strokes until my class has assimilated most of what they need. Why? If I tell you and show you how to do something, you treat it as a straightforward learning experience and simply do it. If I tell you, "Now we'll learn the draw stroke," you'll start thinking something like, "Uh-oh, my buddy says that this is tough," or "Gosh, I've never been able to do this."

It's tough to disguise names in a book, though. Readers like to have landmarks like chapter headings and subheads to help them find their way through a maze of less-than-deathless prose. Okay. Next we're going to talk about the draw stroke. You have thirty seconds to be anxious.

There are two kinds of draw strokes, active and static. The difference is simple. The active draw stroke is our old friend, the power stroke, but here pulling at an angle of up to ninety degrees to the keel line. There are a few subtleties to it, but it's straightforward, and it's a moving stroke; you pull on the paddle. The static draw, which is called a post by marathon racers and a Duffek by whitewater paddlers, is a stationary stroke; you simply hold it in place. We'll use the racer's term post, because it's shorter and communicates better than static draw.

Draw Stroke

"Active draw" sounds like something a busy bartender would do when faced with orders for twelve pitchers of draft from a thirsty crowd of paddlers, doesn't it? We'll just use the term "draw" because we'll be calling the static draw a "post." A draw pulls the canoe toward the side the paddler is paddling on. Either the bow or stern paddler can draw, and it's a powerful correction stroke.

The draw (Figure 3-1) is actually a power stroke, your basic down-and-dirty forward power stroke, but pulling in a different direction. You already know how to do it. Turn your upper body so you're facing the side on which you're paddling. With your arms well away from your

FIGURE 3–1:

Draw stroke.

body and both hands out over the rail, do a forward stroke. Yep, that's right. Pull your end of the canoe sideways using a forward stroke executed perpendicular to the keel line of the canoe. Upper hand high, paddle shaft vertical, and all the body rotation you can muster. This stroke will "draw" the canoe to the paddle, which is why it's called a "draw." Of course, by that reasoning, a forward stroke could be called a "draw" too, because it draws the canoe up to the paddle as well. But then . . . aaah, forget it; this isn't a semantics course.

But I'll tell you one important difference anyway. When you pull on a forward stroke, the paddle is in the water, the canoe is pulled to the paddle and simply moves past it and all is well. When you pull on a draw stroke, your paddle blade is in the water, and the canoe is moving toward it. But . . . WARNING: If you don't do something with the paddle blade, the canoe will run over it, and before you're able to let go of the paddle, you'll be pole-vaulted over the rail and into the water. Your partner will be much amused—unless you also dump the canoe.

There are two ways to avoid this problem. The easiest way is to simply slice the blade out toward your rear by dropping your upper hand forward. This works, but it's not elegant, and no point looking clumsy when you can look good. So, instead of lifting the paddle from the water, keep it in the water and do an underwater recovery for another draw. Here's how. At the completion of the draw, point the thumb of your upper hand away from the boat as close to ninety degrees as you can manage, and push the paddle, with its blade feathered (the paddler's term for "angled") perpendicular to the keel line, back out to the starting position for another draw stroke. Rotate your upper hand back to the power stroke position, and draw again.

Notice that your upper hand hardly moves at all in a draw. It's well outboard of the rail, and essentially stays there in one spot in space and time while you provide power, rotating the shoulder of your lower arm to pull the blade toward you. Notice also that with a bent-shaft paddle, you must place your upper hand well out over the water or the paddle blade will not be vertical and water can slip out underneath your blade, which reduces the effectiveness of the draw stroke.

Post, or Static Draw Stroke

Let's look at how the static draw works. Imagine you're in the bow, paddling along at a modest pace. On a whim—and bow paddlers can indulge in whims—you stick your blade in the water just alongside your hip, blade parallel to the keel line of the canoe so you are looking at the power face of your paddle. Keep the paddle blade as vertical as you can get it. If you're paddling with a straight-shaft paddle, it's easy to keep the blade vertical. But if you have a fifteen bent-shaft stick in your hands, then you're going to have to push that upper hand out over the water far enough to bring the blade to vertical. And that's okay; in fact, to make it work, keep your lower hand close to the canoe. Nothing says this stroke has to be done away from the canoe.

Okay, now what happens? Nothing? You're absolutely right; nothing happens. The blade just slices through the water as cleanly and quietly

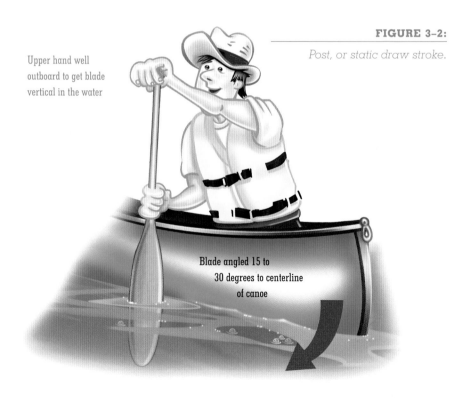

FIGURE 3-2:

Post, or static draw stroke.

Upper hand well outboard to get blade vertical in the water

Blade angled 15 to 30 degrees to centerline of canoe

as you could ask. Now here comes the stroke. Keep the paddle exactly where it is, twist your upper hand back a bit, and "open" the power face of the blade about fifteen to thirty degrees to the oncoming water. The power face will now be "looking" at the oncoming water as you open up your blade.

You will now feel a sideways pull from the paddle, and as the water pushes the paddle away from you, you're hanging on to the paddle so it takes you along with it. And since you are connected to your canoe, the paddle pulls the bow of the canoe to the side as well. Right? Put more angle on the blade, and it pulls you even faster to the side; put less angle on the blade and it moves you sideways more slowly. If you put too much angle on the blade, what happens? The boat slows just as though you'd put a brake in the water. In simple words, a post is nothing more than the initial placement of a draw stroke that is left in place and not pulled toward the canoe. The angled blade slicing through the water moves the bow toward your paddling side.

Before we set aside the post for later use, try turning the angle of the blade the other way. Oops! Did you get wet? I'm sorry. I guess I forgot to mention that if you have the wrong angle on the blade, it will dive under the boat, bang into the side of the canoe, and if you're cruising at speed, may suddenly catapult you into the drink. Practice putting the post into the water with the correct blade angle already set. Do it a few times: power stroke, post, power stroke, post. Soon you'll have it so you don't have to even think about blade angle. And one last tip: When you're finished "posting," simply slice the blade forward in the water and turn it into a power forward stroke. Neat, huh?

Pry Stroke

Some paddle strokes are "antagonistic": What one stroke will do, its antagonistic stroke will undo. The draw has an antagonistic stroke, the pry, which moves a paddler's end of a canoe away from the paddling side. Start with your paddle out of the water, alongside the gunwale with the blade parallel to the side of the canoe and the power face

FIGURE 3–3:

Pry stroke.

Fulcrum on
side of canoe

toward you. Using your lower hand as a fulcrum, raise your upper
hand to slice the blade into the water until the paddle is vertical, keeping the paddle shaft against the side of the canoe. Now simply pull
your upper hand toward you, levering the paddle off the side of the
canoe. You've just used your paddle as a pry bar to move away from
your paddling side, and that's why the stroke is called a pry.

You can see that a pry is less effective with a bent-shaft paddle
than with a straight shaft because the bend of the blade tends to lift
water rather than move the canoe sideways. Since straight-shaft paddlers paddle one side only, the pry becomes the antagonistic response
to the draw. The pry is often used by straight-shaft paddlers in

whitewater. Bent-shaft paddlers switch sides, so rather than use the draw-pry combination, they simply switch sides to use a draw stroke to maneuver the canoe. Nevertheless, there are times when you may find the pry useful, and it should be part of your tool kit. When you're doing a pry with a bent-shaft paddle, carry your upper hand far over the water as you slice the blade into place; that will tuck the blade further under the canoe and give you a more effective pry.

Sweep Stroke

A sweep stroke looks just like you'd think it would. Instead of rotating your upper body and pulling on a vertical paddle parallel to the keel line, you sweep the paddle blade out in an arc, which moves your end of the canoe to the side while still maintaining forward progress. As you

FIGURE 3–4:

Sweep stroke.

FIGURE 3-5:

Overhead view of tandem and solo sweeps.

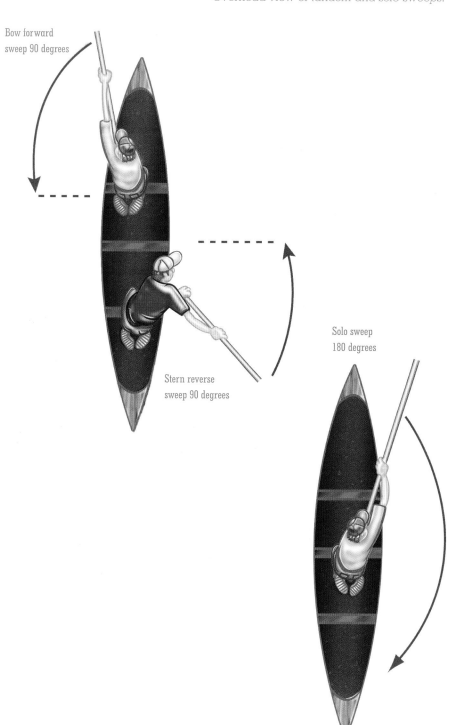

Bow forward
sweep 90 degrees

Stern reverse
sweep 90 degrees

Solo sweep
180 degrees

sweep, focus on keeping your paddle horizontal and reaching out to the side for best leverage.

Don't stab at the water or try to thrash the water to a froth. Maintain the same sort of body rotation you use for your power stroke, with your hands away from your body, and maintain a rhythm. You usually can't sweep at the same tempo you'd maintain for a power stroke, because your paddle blade is in the water over a longer distance. But keep a rhythm and keep smooth. You've probably figured out that you can combine a power stroke and a sweep stroke to get a little of the benefit of each, and you're right. That's true with all your strokes. As you become more proficient and mature as a paddler, you'll be blending them to accomplish exactly what you want. But while you're learning, practice doing the "pure" stroke.

If you're paddling solo, you can sweep from the bow to the stern—180 degrees of arc—and such a stroke will turn you quite nicely. But if you're paddling tandem, and you're in the bow, sweep only in the quadrant from the bow to about ninety degrees to your side. If you're in the stern, sweep from ninety degrees on the side to the stern of the canoe. If you sweep more than that, part of your stroke will actually be counterproductive to your intent.

Now that I've introduced the sweep, remember, please, that most paddle strokes can be done in reverse as well as forward. Try the sweep both forward and backward. (Don't turn your paddle around when you do something backward; just use the other face of the blade.) Try it with the bow sweeping forward and the stern sweeping in reverse, and vice versa. Switch sides and play with the sweep. Get accustomed to powering the stroke with body rotation rather than with your arms. Go for it! Pick a warm day in shallow water and see how much power you can put into the move. So you get wet. You wanted to take a swim anyway, didn't you?

Lift

Both hands out
over water

FIGURE 3-6:

Back stroke.

Backing Up

To backpaddle a canoe using a back stroke, rotate slightly toward the side on which you're paddling, so you start the reverse stroke about where you'd end the forward stroke if you'd over-rotated a bit. Lay the paddle blade horizontally on the surface of the water with both hands out over the water on top of the paddle. Now drive down with your lower hand and lift with your upper hand, rocking your body back so as to provide backing power with your back muscles. Keep the paddle shaft in the vertical plane (both hands over the water) throughout the backing stroke. As your back stroke begins to exit the water, roll your upper hand back and bring it across your body as your lower hand pushes the blade out of the water.

Take note that the bow paddler, in effect, becomes the stern paddler when backpaddling a canoe. Since this new "stern" paddler is facing the wrong way and can't see the overall direction of the canoe, it is difficult to learn to keep a backing canoe under control. But you'll find that by using draws, prys, and reverse sweep strokes, you can get the hang of it. Try it. Paddle backward occasionally just for kicks. Back out of the little duck hole you poked into. Keep at it, have fun with it, and you'll learn to play the game.

J-Stroke

Here's our old friend from Camp Yukintipovurtu, the J-stroke. Hmmm. Must have found that at a flea market. But don't toss it in the corner, my friend. Let's get some of the rust off the old J-stroke and put an edge on it, and we'll find it to be a most useful tool. With bent-shaft paddles, we've been switching sides to keep the canoe running true, but for those with straight-shaft paddles, the J-stroke is the key tool to keep your canoe on course. And it turns out to be useful for the bent-shaft artists who want some extra help keeping those fast, lean canoes on a true course.

Did you ever see one of those J-stroke diagrams in an old canoeing book? There was the J, lying flat, and the counselor told you to do it "just like the book says." So you pulled your butt up to the paddle, pushed out, and performed a short reversing stroke that raised hell with your elbow and just about stopped the canoe in its tracks. But it did keep you on course. Sort of. What you were doing, of course, was compensating for the tendency of the canoe to turn to your opposite side after each stroke. And that's what you'll be doing now, but the old rusty J-stroke is a whole lot sharper, and you don't have to work as hard.

Time was when I wouldn't have used the term "J-stroke," because it was so widely misunderstood. I taught the J-stroke, but I called it a hook stroke, which really describes what it is. But as I grew older and more respectful of tradition, I began calling it the J-stroke again. Besides, the American Canoe Association uses the term, and as an ACA instructor, I'm obliged to use it.

FIGURE 3–7:

J-stroke, as seen from the rear.

Here's how to do it. Just before you complete your power stroke, look at the thumb of your upper hand (on the grip). If your hand is relaxed, the thumb is either lightly touching the edge of the grip, or, if you paddle with a very open hand, as I frequently do, the thumb is pointing almost perpendicular to the keel line of the canoe. It's pointing abeam, if you will. What you need to do to create a small correction in the canoe's course, just enough to almost offset the power stroke, is to give the paddle blade a little twist—the "hook"—and flip outward just before the end of the stroke. Relax your upper hand. Let the thumb point abeam. Just before you finish your power stroke, twist your upper hand so that the thumb points forward. No, it doesn't have to point at the bow paddler. It needn't be that exaggerated. But it should be quick. Immediately after you point that thumb forward, get the paddle out of the water. Don't let it hang there scrubbing off speed. And don't help the process along by rotating your lower hand. Keep your lower hand loose and let the shaft rotate within your grip.

The most skillful J-stroke is the one that makes the smallest correction necessary to keep the canoe tracking straight. That's the most efficient correction, and the one that best maintains the speed of your canoe.

Rudder stroke

I tread sacred ground here. If you are using a straight-shaft paddle, there is another option to maintain your course. It's called a rudder stroke, and may be rejected by some purists. But truth is, a ruddering stroke is somewhat natural. It's how a novice tends to steer a canoe. Begin as if you were intending to use a J-stroke. But instead of turning your upper thumb down, rotate it up, and let the paddle drag like a rudder in the water. With any boat, a rudder works only as long as the boat is moving. The rudder brings your boat back on course, and then you reach forward for the next stroke. This is really a straight-shaft paddle move, and whitewater paddlers use it frequently. Although effective in turning the canoe, the rudder is inefficient because it scrubs off a lot of boat speed. Still, when all else fails, a rudder stroke can help keep your canoe under control.

Will you do these strokes right the first time? No, it takes time. Practice, and crank up the power as you feel more comfortable with your progress. And remember this: Practice produces perfection if you practice perfectly, and perfect practice produces pleasurable paddling. (I've always wanted to say that.)

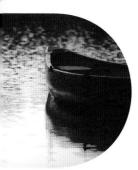

Turning Your Canoe

As the editor of the largest paddling publication in the world, I get the opportunity to teach at a lot of public canoe clinics and symposiums. And it's always surprised me to find so many paddlers who are very concerned about how to turn their canoes, because that's actually the easiest part of boat management. The toughest thing to do with a canoe is to make it run straight and true in a wide range of conditions.

Let's look at what it takes to turn a canoe.

Turning By Not Correcting

The easiest way to make a gradual turn is simply to do nothing. You want to turn right? Stern paddle on the left, bow paddle on the right, don't switch sides, and you'll turn to the right. You've just spent a lot of boat time learning how to keep the canoe from following its natural path, which is to turn. Get out of its way and let it turn!

Want to turn a little faster? Lean the canoe to the outside of the turn, and you'll get a quicker response from your turning strategy. This is easy to do: Since the stern is paddling on the outside of the turn, he or she just leans out a bit. Since you're solidly attached to the canoe (you did install those knee pads, didn't you?), you'll put some outside lean on the hull, which pulls the ends up in the water a little bit and lets the canoe turn more easily.

A couple of hints here. When you have the canoe leaned over a bit, your paddling stroke counteracts the risk of tipping too far—as long as you are pulling on your paddle. As you become more comfortable leaning, you'll find you can lean until the rail is nearly touching the water. But try it on a warm day in shallow water.

The stern paddler can aid a turn by using a sweep stroke instead of a pure forward stroke. (Remember: a stern sweep is done in the quadrant from about ninety degrees to the side all the way back to the stern of the canoe.) To adjust how quickly the canoe turns, use a combination forward/sweep stroke, using more of a sweep if you want to turn faster, more of a forward stroke if you want a lazy turn.

Turning By Paddling On The Same Side

Did I say that? Doesn't this violate Robert's Rule #1? Sure it does, but there are times when even Uncle Harry's rule can be broken, and this is one of them. Now be careful; when you paddle on the same side, you leave the "empty" side vulnerable because no one is at home to brace should the canoe tip in that direction. So you must compensate by keeping the canoe slightly leaned to the side being paddled. The stern paddler is going to have to get both paddles on the same side, either by saying "Hut!" and not changing when the bow changes, or by switching sides without saying "Hut!" at all. Bow paddlers get real nervous when this happens without warning, so sing out "Same side!" before the event. That way, the bow can brace his or her body in the canoe and anticipate the action of the canoe.

Lock yourselves in the boat by flexing your feet against the foot braces. Holding your knees firm against the foam pads on the side, drop the outside hip, and both lean the boat to the outside as you paddle. You'll find the canoe will carve a nice smooth turn, although the canoe itself will wobble with each stroke because the torque produced by each partner isn't cancelled out by paddling opposite sides. If you both sweep, the boat will turn faster. (Bow paddler, remember to sweep in your quadrant from the stem of the canoe to about ninety degrees to the side.) When the turn is complete, the stern either calls "Hut!" or simply switches, whichever is needed to stop the turn and send the canoe back on a straight course again.

Turning With A Post

Turning by not correcting or by paddling on the same side is fine for big, sweeping bends and for course changes on a lake. However, your canoe won't turn quickly. Let's talk about how to turn fast.

We're getting into some real teamwork here. The stern paddler has to call the switch so the bow is paddling on the side to which you want to turn. The bow paddler drops a post stroke—a static draw—in the water while the stern paddler leans the canoe to the outside of the turn and paddles with a sweep. The bow paddler may feel like he's being pulled one way while leaning the other, and that's quite right. But as

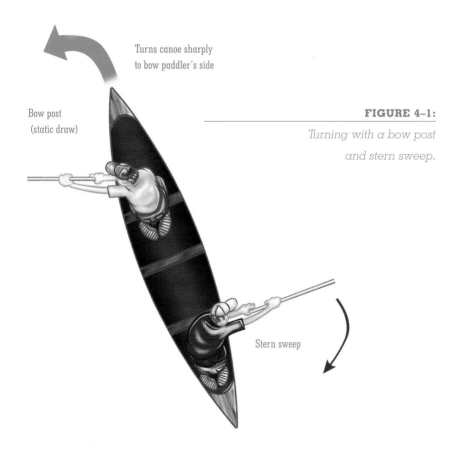

Turns canoe sharply
to bow paddler's side

Bow post
(static draw)

FIGURE 4-1:

*Turning with a bow post
and stern sweep.*

Stern sweep

long as the blade stays in the water and is angled toward the direction of turn, the bow paddler's lean will actually be supported by the paddle as it pulls the bow of the canoe into the turn. (The supportive help is called a brace, which is discussed in Chapter 6). Remember to keep the blade of the post as vertical as possible, which means holding it close to the canoe if you're using a bent-shaft paddle. The angle of the blade will affect how fast the canoe turns, but if you have too much angle, the boat will slow down. As you gain more experience, you will develop a fine compromise between turning speed and boat speed. For now, just remember that if the bow paddle blade produces a gurgling sound during the post, you probably have too much angle on the blade, or the blade isn't vertical in the water.

When you're thinking as a team, the bow can often sense when a limited post is helpful, and simply does it when needed. If the stern paddler needs help with steering, as when fighting a wind, then a simple "Post!" command will alert the bow paddler to assist. Practice this turn until you can lean the rail of your canoe nearly to the water, and you'll learn that you can turn a long tripper even more quickly than you imagined.

As the boat swings into the turn, it starts to turn slowly, and then accelerates. Bow paddler, as you sense the swing of the boat to the completion of the turn, transition your post into a forward stroke by slicing the underwater blade forward, rotating the blade, and then kicking in your power stroke. The boat will fairly blast out of the turn.

I know. You're not a racer. You're not interested in going fast. This isn't about going fast. It's about keeping the boat moving once you've got it moving. Any time you let the boat die in the water unintentionally, you have to crank it back up to a constant pace. It's like the difference in gas mileage between city driving and cruising down I–75, only we're talking about miles per gallon of sweat here.

Using The Active Draw To Turn

You already know that both a post and an active draw stroke move the bow of the boat toward the bow paddler's side. The active draw is a power move; use it when you need to pull the bow over in a hurry. If you don't need to move the bow over right now, don't waste your energy; use a post. If you want to help your stern paddler turn, you can paddle with a combined active draw and a forward stroke, say at forty-five degrees, to maintain headway while also pulling the bow of the canoe into a turn.

Turning Using Straight-Shaft Paddles

In the last chapter we looked at how your J-stroke will keep a canoe tracking straight. If you're using a straight-shaft paddle, the J-stroke becomes the primary tool for turning as well as maintaining course. We've looked at how to turn a canoe by switching sides to take advantage of a canoe's natural propensity to turn when underway. But when paddling with a straight-shaft paddle in the traditional manner, switching sides isn't considered good form, so the J-stroke (or some variation) becomes the tool for turning as well as maintaining course.

If you're using a straight-shaft paddle, you can turn away from the stern paddler's side by not correcting at all, or you can use sweep strokes to accelerate the turn. But when you need to turn toward the side the stern is paddling on, then a pronounced J-stroke is needed to do the job. This scrubs a lot of forward speed, which is why marathon racers took to the sit-and-switch method using bent-shaft paddles.

Whitewater paddlers, who need to make quick and powerful corrections using a straight-shaft paddle, use a horizontal pry off the stern to quickly turn the canoe toward the stern paddling side. To execute this ruddering pry, carry the vertical power stroke well back, keeping it close to the side of the canoe. Twist the paddle by turning the thumb of the upper hand up, and pry off the side of the canoe with a quick push using the back face. (Your paddle blade will be turned so the power face, the side with the piece of tape, is facing you.) Be sure the blade stays in the water so it has something to push against during the last prying portion of the stroke.

Putting Your Tools Into Practice

We've looked at how to make a canoe go straight and how to turn the boat with a post (static draw) or active draw strokes from the bow. You can go straight—no mean accomplishment in these perilous times—and you can turn left and right using a variety of tools. Let's review some of the elements of good turning strokes before we move on. And we will be moving on. There are a few more things you should have in your tool kit before you take that once-in-a-lifetime trip.

Lakeshore Slalom. One of the most pleasant ways to develop boat-handling skills is to paddle the perimeter of a lake, and simply view every dock, every swimming float, every moored boat, every lily pad, and every overhanging branch as an obstacle to be avoided. As you get better and better at this game, try to miss the object by as little a margin as possible. Start with lily pads; they're a lot softer than rocks and docks while you learn and build your confidence. In a short time, you'll find yourself fairly screaming up to an obstruction and snapping the boat around it without scrubbing off hardly any speed at all.

Switching Positions. If possible, practice your new boat-handling skills from both the bow and stern. If you and your paddling partner

One of the most pleasant ways to develop boat-handling skills is to paddle the perimeter of a lake.

can swap positions and still keep the canoe in level trim, change frequently. It helps a lot if your respective weights aren't too different. Paddle a lakeshore slalom; go have some fun. Remember, if you paddle this way you must be able to paddle bow and stern and be comfortable working from both sides of the boat. Be patient. If you've paddled stern all your life, you'll probably be flummoxed by paddling bow with a newcomer in the stern. This is particularly true with husband/wife teams. Be supportive of each other's efforts, please. Be patient, please. You didn't learn to paddle your regular position in a day. Molly and I will switch positions in the boat regularly, sometimes three or four times in a single day of paddling. It keeps us fresh, it gives us different perspective, it lets us use slightly different muscle groups, and it gives us the flexibility to jump in the right seat at the right time to better serve the boat. It also enables us to paddle with anybody who paddles this style. Any time, any river, any paddler.

Initiating Turns. As I've mentioned, this style of paddling requires the bow paddler to be on the side to which the canoe is to be turned, and the stern paddler on the opposite side. There's a good reason for this. An onside turning stroke (one done on your natural paddling side) is more powerful, more easily controlled, more easily turned into a forward stroke, and more stable than a cross-body stroke (crossdraw or crossover). It also keeps the stern paddler in the right position for a bracing move or for other moves to deal with obstacles.

Once you've learned your turning strokes and feel pretty comfortable with them, you'll sooner or later find yourself paddling with a really experienced paddling team. You'll be amazed at how easily they slide their long, fast, touring canoe around obstructions. You're doing well, not to worry. But you know their boat is harder to turn than yours. It's longer and leaner and it doesn't have as much rocker (curvature along the bottom, from bow to stern), and they're aggressive with that boat. They just flat-out scream into turns and make the whole thing look so easy. How can you do that?

They're initiating their turns with a set-up stroke that makes their turning strokes that much more efficient. Let's set up for a right turn. You know the drill: bow on the right, stern on the left. Now when you place a post or a draw, you turn. They place a post or a draw, and the boat fairly snaps around. They may have done several things to initiate the turn and make it more effective. The obvious stroke is a stern sweep done before the bow puts in the draw. More likely, the stern sweeps and the last forward stroke the bow puts in before planting the draw is a forward done maybe thirty degrees off the line parallel to the keel. It's generally called a quarter draw, although it can be at any angle short of ninety degrees to the keel line. This quartering power stroke (or draw stroke—it does a bit of both) sets up the turn while still maintaining momentum into the turn. What does this translate to in terms of energy saving? A good bit, if you're turning a lot, as on a twisty river. It means that you go into the turn faster, carry your speed through the turn, and come out faster. Meanwhile, you've taken four or five fewer strokes in the process. This adds up to a lot more miles per gallon of sweat in the course of a day.

When you've gotten comfortable with these little tricky bits that save your energy and get you across a lake or down a river looking like a pro, we'll show you how to take advantage of moving water in such a way that only the very best paddlers will be able to spot the exact strokes you used to turn your canoe. But that's for later.

For now, go take a run at that dock on the lake, initiate your turn a stroke or two before, and carve a turn around the end of it that will have the folks on the front porch of their cottage standing up and cheering. A touch of the bill of your cap and a short salute is the proper acknowledgment. To ignore applause shows no class.

CHAPTER 5

Maneuvering Your Canoe

Huh? C'mon Uncle Harry! You've been telling me how hard it is to learn to paddle forward, and now you want me to paddle sideways and in circles? Are you sure that's just Gevalia Traditional Roast in your cup?

Believe it. It's just coffee. And you need to know some maneuvers to take care of you in moving water. Sideslips and spins are necessary for boat handling and for moving water. In still water, these skills won't save your boat, but they can save a lot of effort, and they'll have you lookin' good when you need to maneuver your canoe.

Spinning Your Canoe

Remember a few words back when we talked about draws and prys? Have you wondered what happens if both paddlers draw at the same time, or if both paddlers pry at the same time? Well, it's time to find out.

You've followed the bow of your canoe up a small but narrow waterway, and when you get to the end you have to back out or turn around. Canoeists are the sort of folk who prefer to see where they are headed, so how are you going to turn around? What if you both reach out to the paddling side and do an active draw stroke? Each paddler is pulling an end of the canoe toward his or her paddling side, and because

FIGURE 5–1:

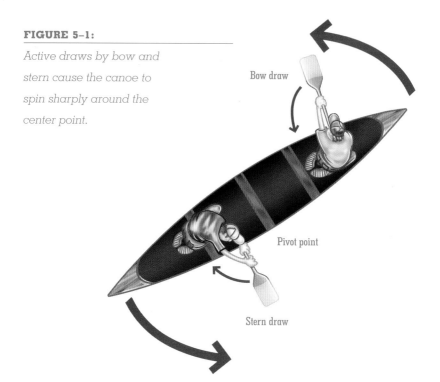

Active draws by bow and stern cause the canoe to spin sharply around the center point.

Bow draw

Pivot point

Stern draw

you're on opposite sides, the boat will spin around the center yoke, and you're on your way home. Almost too simple, isn't it?

As usual there's a couple points to consider. If you pull ninety degrees to the keel line, the canoe will spin. But if you want to spin with a little more efficiency, the bow paddler should reach back a little more than ninety degrees, and the stern paddler should reach a little forward of ninety degrees. Now you're pulling yourself in the exact direction that you travel on the circle defined by the spin. Try it, play with it, and while you're at it, check to see if your canoe is spinning around a single point or going forward or back while you're spinning. Practice until you can "spin on a dime"—as long as the dime is set in the center of your center yoke.

Want to spin the other way? No problem. You can switch sides and use draw strokes, or you can each pry your end of the canoe away from your paddling side. The pry approach isn't used so much by bent-shaft paddlers, since this paddling style switches sides for control. Besides, a bent-shaft paddle doesn't pry very well because the angled blade tends to lift up water rather than push the canoe to the side. But if you're using straight-shaft paddles, spinning with paired pry strokes is quite powerful, even though not as quick as using draw strokes.

Want to improve timing for paddling in sync? Then spin! If you're in perfect unison placing your paddle in the water, pulling, and exiting the water, your canoe will spin silky smooth. If you're just a little bit off, it will wobble like a car with a flat tire. When you both can reach out and spin with draw strokes, leaving a (plastic) cup of water on your yoke without spilling, you've got it.

Sideslipping Your Canoe

Here's the situation. You're paddling the classic Adirondack Canoe route from Old Forge to the Saranacs (or to Tupper Lake, which is how I always preferred to end it). You've carried from Raquette Lake (it was windy, wasn't it?) into Forked Lake, and you've ridden a crisp westerly down the lake to the shallow, rocky outlet so you can register for a campsite with the ranger. You're zipping along at a good clip, and there's a large granite boulder a few boat lengths dead ahead and four inches under the water. The water's gin-clear, but the waves were busy enough that you didn't notice it. What do you do?

You can backpaddle, and you'll probably stop in time to avoid the ego-deadening "thunk" that says "You blew it!" to the whole universe. But with a loaded canoe, a good head of steam, and a following wind, you

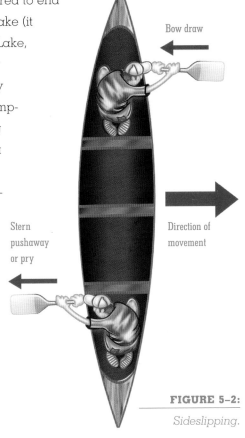

Bow draw

Direction of movement

Stern pushaway or pry

FIGURE 5–2:
Sideslipping.

might not stop in time. You could turn, but the wind and waves might slow the turn enough for the stern to slide into or onto the rock.

Help!

Help is on its way. Bow paddler, stick in a draw, a hard draw. Stern paddler, your bow paddler has just put in a hard draw, and you don't know why. Trust your bow paddler. Your bow paddler wouldn't do that out of a clear blue sky; there must be something up there that imperils the canoe. Don't think. Don't analyze. Push the stern of the canoe away from your paddle so that the canoe is moving forward and sideways, bow and stern aligned. If your bow puts in another draw, just keep pushing the stern away from the paddle, and keep doing it until the bow drops back into a forward traveling stroke.

Whew! That was close! You missed the boulder, and the canoe's still zipping along with minimal loss of speed. Now's the time to back-paddle. It gets quite rocky here, and you'll have to pick your way through to the takeout at the ranger station. So you just sideslipped your canoe, which is exactly what the name says: slipping the boat sideways to avoid an obstacle.

Pushaway Stroke

Now let's look at what you just did as a team. The bow paddle moved the boat sideways with an active draw stroke. If there had been a boat length more warning, the bow may simply have chosen a post (or static draw). The stern did the reverse of an active draw, a stroke called a pushaway. It's not an easy stroke to learn. It goes against all your common sense to move strongly away from the boat. Until you have the pushaway down solidly, remember that a reverse sweep will also push the canoe away from the paddle. The drawback to the reverse sweep is that it slows the canoe down more than the pushaway. If you come from a whitewater tradition or a classic tradition, you could use a pry stroke. I prefer the pushaway for touring paddlers using bent-shaft paddles.

Why the pushaway? A couple of reasons. It's smoother than the pry, and there are times when smooth is important. It leaves you in a position to move directly into another stroke, be it another pushaway, a brace, or a forward stroke. And because the power phase of the push-away is about the same length as the power phase of the draw, the boat doesn't wiggle and jiggle. It feels stable at a point where you may very well need that feeling of stability. Let's look at the mechanics of a pushaway.

If you think of the pushaway as a reverse power stroke done ninety degrees to the keel line of the canoe, you won't go wrong. You know how to do a draw in the stern. Instead of starting the blade well away from the canoe as in a draw, start the pushaway with your torso nearly parallel to the keel line, and the paddle close to the boat. Slice the blade from behind until fully submerged with the power face (on a straight-shaft paddle, the side with the tape) facing you. Apply power by rotating your upper body, directing the thrust away from the canoe with your lower arm and back. If you start with the paddle blade verti-cal, then your upper hand will be out over the water to begin. As you rotate the shoulder of your lower hand outward, remember that you're pivoting around the point of your upper hand's shoulder. Your upper hand hardly moves at all. The entire stroke is no longer than a draw; you don't have to end with your body hanging out over the rail.

To recover, you can slice the paddle out of the water or you can feather (angle) the paddle blade just like you did with the draw, except now you're returning the blade to the boat feathered. Do the stroke again if you need to. One pushaway in the stern for each draw in the bow is the rule of thumb, and please try to do the strokes together. Stern, watch your bow! Trust your bow. Follow your bow.

An Aside

Guys, if you're paddling with your wife or that special friend in the bow, here's the instance that shows whether you're a paddler or Captain Macho. If you missed the rock, you both did your job. If you hit the rock, you both blew it. There is room in a canoe for a lot of things. Pierre

Berton once observed that a Canadian is somebody who can make love in a canoe, and the irrepressible Philip Chester capped Mr. Berton's observation by noting that one must know how to remove the center thwart. Room enough indeed! But there is never room enough in a canoe for placing blame. There's room for figuring out what went wrong, and there's room for learning, but there's never room in a canoe for placing blame. Not in our canoe, and not in your canoe if you want to paddle with us.

Keeping the Water Out

When you get right down to it, Steve Scarborough is right. There aren't many things you have to do with a canoe. You have to make it go forward and backward, turn it right and left, move it sideways, and keep the river in its proper place, which is outside and beneath the canoe. In a fair and just world, if you can make the canoe go forward and back, turn right and left, and move sideways, you've accomplished ninety-eight percent of what you have to do to keep the river in its place. Let me bore you with a story.

Back when Molly and I ran two outdoor shops and a cross-country ski area, we taught paddling a lot, both kayaking and canoeing. In winter the introductory kayaking classes were conducted in a swimming pool, because in upstate New York water is frequently stiff in January and February. It took what could euphemistically be called "force of character" to keep the novice kayakers on track. They'd all come from a canoeing background and were incensed by the idea that we wanted them to learn to control their boats before we started teaching them to roll up. They finally got the idea that good paddling skills and sound mechanics would enable them to control their boats in such a way that they might not have to roll up as often. Bingo!

I'll show you two strokes that will keep the river in its

place. Just remember that the better you manage all the other strokes, the less likely you'll need these.

The Low Brace

The basic "Ohmigod!" stroke for canoeists and kayakers alike is the low brace. The common image of the stroke is one of a paddler falling on his paddle with a resounding slap that sounds like a beaver on steroids. The proper image to fix in your mind is a quick, subtle move that's mostly done by body position and that flows directly into a stroke. It's easier to learn a low brace in a solo canoe or in a tandem canoe paddled solo from amidships. This doesn't mean that you can't learn it in a tandem canoe; you just have to maintain good rapport with your partner.

Here's how it works. Hold the paddle as if you were taking a forward stroke, then place it horizontally, the knuckles of your lower hand down, the back face (no tape) of the blade flat to the water, away from

FIGURE 6-1:

Low brace.

Fulcrum hand

the canoe and out beside your hips. Your upper hand should be about at your belly button, your body comfortably erect and elbows slightly bent. Now lean on the paddle and push down into the water. Start with a slight lean, and increase it as you feel comfortable. Recover by lifting your upper hand. Why? If you push down against the water with your lower hand, your weight will be too far outboard for the small paddle blade to support you. The blade will sink, with you attached to it.

When you lift your upper hand, your body moves against the roll of the boat and rights it. The paddle does very little beyond giving you a moment's purchase against which to move your body. Whether sitting or kneeling, to aid body movement, focus on driving your outboard knee up, while lowering the opposite hip. Once you have the mechanics of which hand to move under control, do it some more, but this time drop your head and shoulders to lower your roll center. Works better, eh? No surprise. You shortened the lever arm that wants to roll you over.

Let's get braver. Let your upper hand move farther and farther outboard as you practice, until both hands are outboard of the canoe's rails. Try to get the knuckles of your upper hand wet, and then the wrist. Drop your head and shoulders down inside the rails. Great! Your canoe was tipped far enough over to take in water, and you braced back up smoothly!

But sooner or later, you won't make it. You needed one more brace, but the paddle sank out of sight before you could do it, and took you with it. For a simple low brace, with your upper hand inboard at about your belly button, recovering the paddle is easy. For those times when the going is tough, you must get the paddle back to the surface so you can either brace again or move directly into an active stroke. As you lift your upper hand, turn it so your thumb points upward about thirty degrees, and rotate your upper body slightly toward the bow. This will drive the paddle in what looks and feels like a very short, powerful reverse sweep with the power directed downward. The blade will climb to the surface, and you're ready to brace again or move the canoe forward or sideways. This move is called a sweeping low brace by some.

This is fine—so far. Either paddler can and must be able to brace from either side of the boat and from either bow or stern. It's obvious that the stern paddler is in a position to execute a more powerful brace than the bow, but the boat doesn't always roll to the stern paddler's side. What do you do if you're the offside paddler? The simplest thing you can do is drop your head and shoulders to lower the roll center of the boat, and brace on your side. This gets your weight low and over the offside rail, and your paddle ready to catch the boat when it rolls back up.

If you're really hard-core about learning to brace, pick a warm day on a warm lake with a sandy bottom. Have a friend stand waist-deep in the water at the stern of your canoe and provide some unpredictable wave action for you. You need a solid brace most of all when you're not expecting it.

The High Brace

This is a classic maneuver. It's pretty, graceful, effective, and can be easily turned into a draw or a forward stroke. Most paddlers think of it as a bow stroke, but it works in the bow or the stern.

The high brace looks almost like our friend the static draw stroke (see Chapter 3), with a couple of differences. Draws, either static or active, are done with your upper torso rotated so you can face your work, as it were. You don't always have the time to do that when you need a brace. The paddle shaft is vertical or nearly so when you draw, because a draw is really a power stroke put in ninety degrees to the keel line of the canoe. On the other hand, a high brace is usually done with the shaft angle more like forty-five degrees to the water than ninety degrees, and the power of the stroke is directed both down and toward the boat rather than toward the boat alone.

The active part of the brace, the part in which you're exerting force on the paddle blade, is very short. The high brace is a favorite of sea kayakers and whitewater kayakers, because it's really a part of their Eskimo roll. (You could make a strong case that the roll is nothing more than a high brace done from a very awkward position.) At any rate, you can tip a kayak to ninety degrees and the river won't come in. You can't do that with an open boat. The best application of the high brace in an open boat is to impart a short-term steadying factor as you look for the right time to power out, turn, or sideslip. It's a particularly comfortable stroke for the bow paddler, because the bow paddler must always be prepared to apply power or set up a turn, and it's always easier to do those things from the firm platform of a high brace.

You may have noticed that a high brace doesn't always have to be a "high" stroke and the low brace isn't always done "low," though such is often the case. What really differentiates them is the paddle face that applies the power to the stroke. The high brace is a power-face stroke, whereas a low brace is a pushing stroke using the back face of the paddle.

To avoid confusion: As we've already discovered, sit-and-switch paddlers call the high brace a post, because it acts very much like a post that a bow paddler grabs to turn the canoe. If you take a paddling course from an instructor certified by the American Canoe Association (ACA), the high brace will be called a static draw or a Duffek, in honor

FIGURE 6–2:

High brace.

Pulls canoe
back upright

of the Czech wizard who developed it. This isn't a new term; neither is it a new stroke. But both the term and the stroke have been used primarily in open boat whitewater instruction, rather than in open canoe touring. The change in nomenclature is logical, and promotes a greater accuracy in talking about stroke mechanics.

Practice, Practice, Practice!

Go from a hanging draw to a forward power stroke to a low brace. Vary the sequence; blend your strokes. You should, in time, be able to go from any stroke to any other stroke—which well may include switching sides—with absolute ease, and without thinking about it. Paddling a canoe is blending the various strokes in your tool kit to take care of the boat. Remember: The only stroke you'll ever take that isn't part of a sequence is the last one you take when you come to shore.

Canoeing in Wind and Waves

It always struck me as strange that all canoeing books spend countless pages telling you how to paddle moving water and whitewater, yet ignore how to paddle in wind and waves. The skills are related, in the sense that good stroke mechanics, a calm demeanor, bone-deep teamwork, and a boat suited to the environment are essential. What makes paddling in wind and waves different? Several things.

To begin with—and maybe even to end with—there aren't any eddies on a big, windswept bay. You can't pop behind a rock in the current and find a little patch of calm in which to take a deep breath and make a plan for approaching what lies downstream. If you blow it, there's a long, long swim in store. It may not be as violent a swim as a heavy rapid gives, but sooner or later, even the worst rapid deposits you in a calm pool. Lakes end at the shoreline, and a half-mile swim in the forty-two-degree water of Lake Superior into the teeth of a wind is serious business. Finally, wind waves move; river waves are generally stationary. Lake water stays in one place; lake waves move. River water moves; river waves stand still.

There's one rule governing all big-water paddling. Write it indelibly on the back of your hand; chisel it into your memory. If it's bad now, it will probably get worse. Stay on shore or get to shore and wait it out. Yes, there are exceptions to this rule. You'll learn those exceptions as you grow in skill, experience, and wisdom. I grew up on a big lake. I live a half-mile by river from a very big lake, Lake Huron. I've spent a lot of time paddling in the Gulf of Mexico and other such bodies of water. And my partner, Molly, is as good a wind and wave paddler as you'll find anywhere. Yet we always have a couple of books and the binoculars and a bird guide with us for those days when we say, "No way!" Maybe we could have paddled. If we were in an emergency situation, like one of our party having had a heart attack, we would have paddled and probably made it. But we paddle for pleasure. And while it's fun to push the envelope sometimes—if the water's warm and the boat's empty—four hours of living on the edge in a survival situation isn't what most folks are seeking.

Paddling Upwind

Most paddlers get worried at the thought of running upwind, bucking the waves. But one advantage of paddling upwind is that you can see the waves coming, and you can paddle actively rather than reactively. If the waves aren't high, the simplest strategy is to run right up the gut and deal with them head-on. This puts a lot of spray in your bow paddler's face, and the boat loses speed because it's pitching up and down as much as it's going forward, but it has the charm of simplicity and it feels most predictably stable. The artist's way is to take the waves at an angle when they're high and run up into them at each momentary lull. Waves are never uniform. They'll come in sets of big ones and smaller ones, and sometimes you can find a relatively "flat" section that you can just hammer through.

When running straight upwind, switch sides frequently to flush the fatigue products from your muscles. You're working hard when you paddle upwind; do what you can to ease the fatigue. Learn to adjust the stroke cadence to match the cycle of the waves in order to smooth out the bouncing action of the canoe as much as possible. As you grow more skilled and start attacking waves at angles when the opportunity presents itself, keep the stern on the downwind side of the canoe and the bow upwind. This puts the bow in position to draw up into the wind

One advantage of paddling upwind is that you can see the waves coming and can paddle actively rather than reactively.

and waves as needed, and causes the stern's forward stroke to naturally drive the bow of the boat into the wind to keep from turning sideways and wallowing in the trough of the wave (broaching).

Quartering up into waves is a little more wiggly that running them head-on. The orbital motion of water particles in the crest of a wave are moving against the canoe at the time when the bow is most fully buried, and the canoe tends to be moved off a level orientation by the slope of the wave face. You've added another component of motion—roll—to the pitch component you deal with when running straight upwind.

If the waves are big and your course is upwind, a quartering strategy can help keep the water out of the canoe. The stern paddler should not only be paddling on the lee side of the canoe, but have a dependable bracing stroke. As the bow heads up the oncoming wave face, lean away from the oncoming wave, knowing that the wave crest wants to overturn the canoe the same way you're leaning. The stern paddler hits a forward/sweeping stroke as the wave hits, both to maintain the bow from being knocked off course and to brace from overturning. The lean away from the oncoming wave produces a greater hull surface to absorb the wave, keeping water out of the canoe. Just be sure that the bracing stroke is on time and solid, or you will help the wave overturn the canoe.

Paddling Downwind

Looks like fun, eh? You've just left the dock at Clearwater Lodge in Minnesota's Boundary Waters Canoe Area, fueled with anticipation and Clearwater's pancakes. You dawdled over coffee (you always dawdle over coffee at Clearwater Lodge), and the prevailing westerlies are already dappling the big lake with catspaws, even at the lee shore. Wow! This is going to be an easy ride down to the 214-rod portage into West Pike!

Well maybe not. Paddling a following sea with comfort and aplomb is one of the high points of the art. What should be a piece of cake can be turned into a horror show. A canoe running down the face of a wave gains speed rapidly, propelled by wind, wave, and the orbital flow of the wave itself. And when the canoe hits the trough of the wave, the bow buries, the canoe starts to run uphill, the orbital motion of the wave restrains its passage, and the stern half of the canoe is still accelerating. You're about to become a submarine—unless you're paddling a little off the wind. Then, the stern will swing crosswise as it slides down the face of the wave. Oh, my, Maynard, you told me this would be easy! What are we going to do?

First, relax. If you're stiff, your head and shoulders are so much dead weight at the end of a three-foot lever arm that does nothing but raise the roll center of the canoe at a time when you least want a high roll center. Let the canoe roll under you as you paddle, using your hips and foot braces to keep control while your upper body rolls loosely and stays centered over your hips. (Now aren't you really glad you installed those foam knee pads in the canoe?) You can roll a canoe right up to the rail with no consequence if your nose is over your hips and relaxed. Stiffen up, and you're swimming for sure! Enjoy the sleigh ride. Revel in it and in your control of the situation. Paddle with the calm of a Zen

When paddling downwind let the canoe roll under you as you paddle, using your hips and foot braces to keep control while your upper body rolls loosely and stays centered over your hips.

archer shooting out the flame of a candle. Feel the waves act on the canoe. Roll with them.

Strategies? In a following sea, bow maintains way, stern maintains direction. Switches are always called by the stern paddler—and don't expect many. The stern generally paddles on the lee side of quartering waves, because a ruddering pry or reverse sweep will keep the canoe from sliding down the face of the wave and broaching in the trough. This also puts the stern on the side most likely needing a brace. Keep the canoe from accelerating (surging) down the face of a wave, keep it from stalling in the trough of a wave, and keep it from spinning on top of a wave as the wave bears under its middle, and you'll do just fine. Get in tune with the corkscrew action of quartering waves so you can anticipate the motion and enjoy the ride. Don't just drift through following seas, though. If you're moving at wave speed, you're at the mercy of the waves. Be more aggressive as your skills improve. Too much enthusiasm may sometimes get you into trouble, but too little enthusiasm will always get you into trouble.

Paddling In Beam Seas

Paddling across the waves requires the greatest degree of "feel" of all big-water paddling modes, because there's more happening to the canoe in a beam sea.

Objects in the water tend to make the same motion as the water they displace. A canoe in a beam sea (i.e., a canoe traveling across the waves, or, at a right angle to the wind) will follow the same circular motion as the orbiting particles in the wave that moves beneath it. There's not much relative motion between the canoe and the water, and an empty canoe would not likely be swamped in this situation. But, add paddlers to the canoe, and the roll center is well above the waterline. This isn't a problem either, if you stay relaxed and fluid as the wave slips underneath. If you can't, the slight lean change that the canoe assumes—leaning leeward on the wave face, leaning windward on the back of the wave, and passing through a neutral point at the crest and the trough—will be magnified. Remember this: The canoe will easily change from a leeward lean to a windward lean before the relatively high and heavy mass of your body will. Roll with the wave, using your hips to absorb the motion of the canoe as the wave passes underneath.

Physical law plays a big part here. It doesn't take a huge sea to wreak havoc. One of the two worst seas to take abeam is a sea whose crests are twice the waterline width of the canoe. Why? Because the wave period is so short that the canoe quickly passes through the leeward, windward, and neutral zones and the rate of roll is difficult to adjust to. And that's not a spectacular sea! For an average 17- to 18-foot canoe with a waterline width of 34 inches, this situation will occur at a wave height of about 10 inches in deep water, because a 10-inch wave will have a period (length from crest to crest) of about 68 inches.

The other worst wave to take abeam is a breaking wave, partly because the breaking wave violates the predictable orbital motion. The canoe starts to rise on the wave face and leans to leeward, and then gets hammered by water falling from the crest of the breaking wave. It doesn't take a lot of imagination to figure out what happens next! You've got a problem: You can either lean away from the breaking crest and the wave will overturn you, or you can lean toward the crest to remain stable, but take the breaking water into the canoe. If you're really good, and a little bit lucky, you can split the middle and avoid both problems.

How to paddle in a beam sea? Stay loose. I know; you've heard that before. I meant it then and I mean it now. Enjoy, enjoy, enjoy. Keep the stern paddler on the leeward side, the bow on the windward. This keeps the effective brace where it needs to be, and also positions the bow paddler for the option to draw up into and over the wave crest and run for a set of smaller waves.

In big waves, it's sometimes useful to lean the canoe a bit to the lee side. This is a bit like weighting the downhill ski; your senses rebel against the notion. But it's a way to keep big waves and breaking waves from dropping into the canoe. Stay alert. Nasty, steep, short-period waves can be run by quartering into them as you head for the bigger but longer-period stuff to run in the trough. It may seem more intimidating, but it's a smoother ride.

It's worth remembering that different hull shapes react differently to beam seas (Figure 7-1). A canoe with a flat bottom (left) reacts very

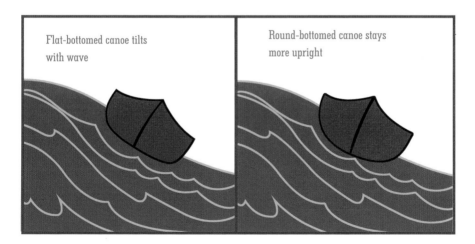

Flat-bottomed canoe tilts with wave

Round-bottomed canoe stays more upright

FIGURE 7-1:

Different hull shapes in beam seas.

quickly to a wave and follows the contour of the wave, which can put the canoe in a very unstable position. A more rounded hull has less freeboard (hull above the water line) but reacts more slowly and will ride out a wave in a more upright position.

Hints

Dave Getchell Sr., a wonderfully sensible man, once offered us some wonderfully sensible advice. If the wind is kicking up to where paddling is a problem, and there's a shoreline that permits it, tow the canoe along the shore. It never occurred to me, so help me. I've had occasion to use that advice since, and it works. Also, if you have to round a narrow point, and the waves look like killers off the point, head for shore and see if you can portage across the point and put in on sheltered water. Avoiding a problem is always a better alternative than working your way out of a problem. That's just as true for paddling a canoe.

CHAPTER 8

Canoeing in Moving Water

This isn't a book about whitewater; neither is it a book about river reading. It's a book about paddling technique. But you won't be paddling very long before you encounter moving water. There are some things you should know about stroke combinations and how to handle a canoe in moving water so you can pass through safely and with confidence. Bent-shaft paddles are the easiest and most efficient way to paddle a canoe in flatwater, and can be used in moving water. However, if you progress to faster and more difficult water, straight-shaft paddles better execute the draw and pry strokes that are the backbone of maneuvering a canoe in whitewater.

Ferrying

A ferry is a maneuver that uses river current to move a canoe sideways across a river. You can ferry across moving water with the canoe facing upstream (upstream ferry, Figure 8-1) or downstream (backferry). An upstream ferry is generally associated with whitewater. However, for those of us who view upstream paddling against a stiff current as an art form, mastering an upstream ferry is fun and feels good, gets you places that you might not otherwise get to, and obviates the need for a shuttle, because you can paddle upstream by yourself, turn around and return to your starting point.

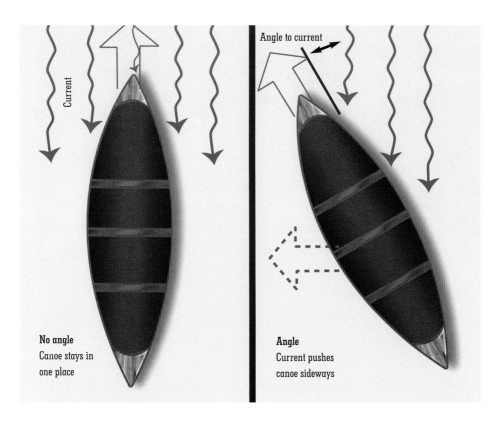

FIGURE 8–1:

Upstream ferry angle.

Paddling upstream may seem foreign to a beginner, but the upstream ferry is easier to execute than the downstream. Balance the power of your strokes to the speed of the current. To ferry across the river, simply put a ten- to twenty-degree angle between your boat and the current, pointing the bow toward the direction you wish to ferry. The stern paddler adjusts and controls this angle in the same manner as setting an overall course on a flat lake. Notice I said the angle is relative to the current. Some paddlers assume a river's current runs straight between parallel banks. It doesn't. Current direction in rivers is ever changing, and you'll have to adjust your angle to match changes in current direction. As the river current carries you across, throw in a little downstream lean to keep the big bad current from piling up on the upstream side of your canoe hull, and you're good to go.

Speed, angle, and lean are the common components of every ferry maneuver. The bow paddler's responsibility is to maintain speed against the oncoming current. The stern paddler is responsible for maintaining correct angle with the current, primarily by using draws and prys, although sweeps may work as well. When you're first learning, it's easier if the bow paddler paddles on the upstream side of the ferry while the stern paddler paddles on the downstream side. The canoe is most easily leaned by whomever is paddling on the side toward the lean, so the stern paddler is in better position to lean the canoe away from the oncoming current. Correction strokes to maintain the proper ferry angle with the current are also easier if the stern paddler is on the side toward which the canoe is ferrying.

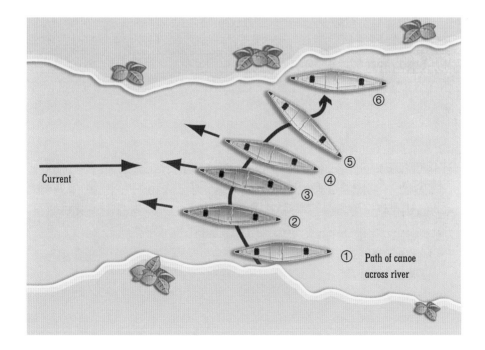

FIGURE 8-2:

Upstream ferry across a river.

When paddling upstream the bow paddler should call the switches loudly over their shoulder so the stern paddler can hear them.

There's really no difference between an upstream ferry and a downstream (back) ferry except for the different direction of the canoe and the fact that a backferry changes the responsibilities of the bow and stern paddlers. To backferry, both paddlers will have to use effective back strokes to hold the canoe in place in the moving current. (This might be a good time to review your back stroke technique from Chapter 3. Focus on using your back to get power in your back stroke, and keep that paddle vertical during the stroke.)

Now the bow paddler becomes the steersman for purposes of setting and controlling the angle with the current. You'll find it easiest for the bow to be paddling on the upstream side and the stern on the downstream side. Here's a case where the bow paddler will call the switches if any are to be made. Make sure they're over the shoulder and loud so your stern paddler can hear. The ferry principles are the same—speed, angle, and lean—but since you're "backward," backferrying tends to be confusing at first. Remember that the stern paddler becomes the new "bow" and should be pointed toward the direction you wish to move. A backferry can be more difficult to execute because most canoeists are not adept at paddling backwards. Also, when paddling backwards, it's difficult for the bow paddler, facing forward, to watch the alignment of the canoe with the current.

You can practice ferries anywhere there's moving water. Start with slow current at first. It's neat. It's fun. It will feel funny the first few times you do it, because your eyes will play tricks on you. It almost makes some people light-headed the first few times they do it. But once you've mastered the upstream and downstream ferries, you've bought yourself a huge chunk of freedom on the river.

Eddy Turns

You can use variations in river current to help you turn the canoe with surprisingly little effort. In fact, you can use the current to make a long,

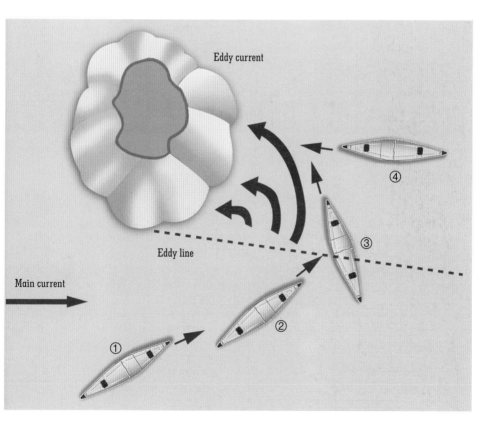

FIGURE 8-3:

Eddy turn.

lean, mean tourer fairly dance down a twisty little stream while your clueless friends are picking themselves out of the weeds.

Poke the nose of the canoe into a part of the stream that's moving slower than the patch of water you're riding, and see how fast the current will swing the canoe around. It's great fun, and it's your best way to stop for lunch or to scout out what's ahead on the river. Find enough current differential, such as you might find behind a big rock or on the inside of a sharp turn, and the stern paddler will feel like he or she's playing "crack the whip" on skates.

An eddy turn (Figure 8-3) has the same elements as a ferry: speed, angle, and lean. Before you get to the turn, set up your paddling sides with the bow paddling on the inside of the anticipated turn, stern paddling on the outside. Approach that slower-moving water with enough speed to move across the eddy line (the seam separating the fast

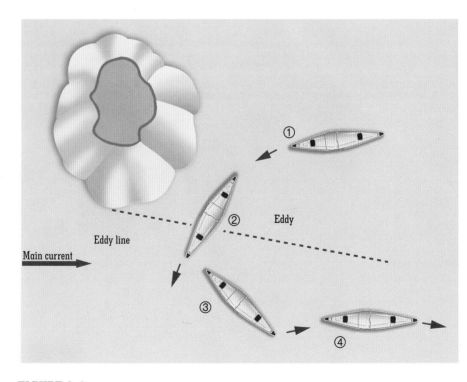

FIGURE 8-4:

Peel-out.

water from the slow), but not so fast as to push the canoe all the way into the slow water before the current differential has time to act on the canoe. You should anticipate an angle to the eddy line of about forty-five to sixty degrees. Enter at ninety degrees, and the sudden change of current may jerk your bow to the side more quickly than you can react. Enter at more than ninety degrees, and you really are ferrying into the eddy, not turning.

As the bow enters quieter water in the eddy, the bow paddler plants a post (static draw) in the quiet water. Plant deep, and make sure the blade has plenty of angle. The bow paddler leans into the turn, making sure the canoe hull is leaned as well. A lot can go wrong on a snappy eddy turn, but a solid boat lean will cover a lot of sins. Hold the lean until the turn is fully complete. This, simply stated, is the way you enter an eddy. River runners call it "eddying out." You can use minor variations in current speed to help you turn on any stream. Play it just right, and nobody will figure out how you're doing it!

You can exit an eddy and continue downstream using a maneuver called a peel-out (Figure 8-4). Enter the current with some speed, with the canoe at a forty-five-degree angle to the eddy line. The bow paddler should be paddling on the downstream side, the side you will be turning to. Drive briskly across the eddy line, with the bow leaning the canoe into the turn and placing a post (static draw) in the downstream river current. You will feel much more stable during the turn if the canoe is leaned before the bow crosses the eddy line. As you cross the eddy line, the boat and bow paddle will be caught by the current, and the canoe will swing downstream. Once the turn is complete, reduce the lean, pour on the power, and you're on your way.

Classical whitewater technique for peel-outs is a bit cleaner, and may be the only excuse for a touring paddler to learn a cross-bow stroke (Figure 8-5), which keeps the stern paddling on the inside of the turn in a better position to brace.

A word about speed, eddy turns, and canoe design. You may think you're doing the turning with your strokes, but you're just helping the river. It's the current differential that actually turns the canoe. If you go too slow

FIGURE 8–5:

Leaving an eddy using a cross-bow draw stroke.

across the eddy line, you won't get the bow into the "other" water in time and you'll miss the eddy or the current. If you go too fast, you'll slice the whole canoe across the eddy line before the current differential has time to work on turning your boat. You'll become proficient at estimating how much speed is required for a particular eddy line as you practice. A longer, leaner boat takes longer to turn than a short canoe with pronounced rocker (i.e., with more curve from stem to stem), and will need more time on the eddy line, which translates into less speed.

One more word about lean. Lean downstream when on a ferry. Lean into the turn (like a bicycle cornering) when you do eddy turns. Hold the lean until the turn is complete. There, I've said it twice. If you need to hear it a third time, the river will do the talking, and when the river speaks, you get wet!

Running A Bend

Ever seen a perfectly straight river? Not likely. Meanders are part of the defining character of rivers. So you're going to have to deal with bends. On any river, current flows to the outside of a bend, and if there are trees along that outside bank, it's just a matter of time until the current erodes the bank and drops a tree into the water. The same current that cut down the tree will try to sweep you into the tree. The downed tree is called a strainer, and it's a good thing to encounter only if you have gills. Sometimes a tree will be hanging over the water about canoe level (a sweeper), and sometimes trees and debris will pile up in a log jam. You're going to have to find a way to run a bend that keeps you and your boat away from strainers, sweepers, and log jams on the outside of bends.

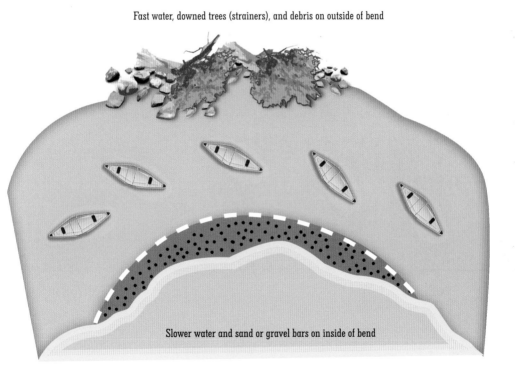

Fast water, downed trees (strainers), and debris on outside of bend

Slower water and sand or gravel bars on inside of bend

FIGURE 8–6:

Running a bend.

You already have one of the tools; it's the backferry. Approaching the bend, begin slowing the canoe with back strokes, and set an angle with the stern of the canoe pointed to the inside of the turn. As you backferry, the current will slide you to the relative safety of the inside bank. Here's where practice pays off; you can't afford to miss on your backferry if failure risks putting your boat into the obstruction.

There's another, more aggressive way to run a bend. As you approach the bend, begin to point the bow of the canoe toward the inside of the bend. As you continue paddling forward—keeping the bow pointed toward the inside of the bend—the river current will sweep you toward the outside of the bend, but you will power yourself away from the outside bank and any danger that it holds. It's not unlike accelerating a car out of a four-wheel drift through a turn on a gravel road. The beauty of this approach is that you are setting yourself up for an eddy turn into the eddy that is always found on the inside of a river bend. If you need to stop for a break or for scouting, you're already set up; if not, scrub it off, turn downstream, and continue on.

A final crucial rule: Don't ever go around a bend unless you can see a clear channel continuing on downstream, or a definite place where you know you can stop. If you're uncertain, put the boat on the bank, get out, and take a look. River runners say it succinctly: "When in doubt, scout."

Upstream Paddling

Here's where you use of lot of the strokes you've learned, and use them powerfully and wisely. The upstream ferry is a necessity, because you'll need to slide from side to side to take the path of least resistance. High and low braces are needed because this is moving water and it exerts surprising force on your canoe. And you'd best be able to paddle forward with power, switch sides without missing a beat, and work as a team without finding fault with each other.

You need not be a Top Gun candidate to look at a fast-moving river and see where the slower-moving water is. It's downstream of

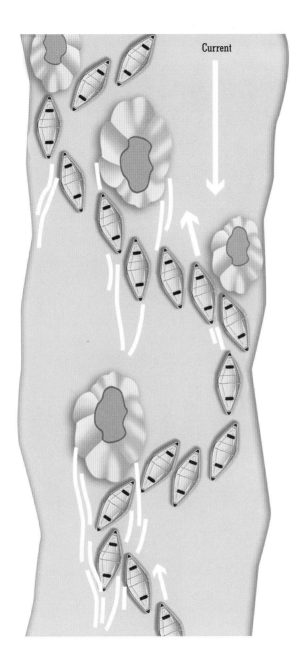

FIGURE 8–7:

Working upstream.

obstructions like logs and rocks. It's along the shoreline, more so to the inside of a bend than the outside. Sometimes, if the river is fast enough, the slow-water stretches along the shoreline are actually flowing upstream. When traveling upstream (Figure 8-7), you want to seek out slow-moving water, and if you can slip your canoe into those eddies, you can catch a free upstream ride. It takes boat-handling skills and experience to ferry back and forth, find an eddy here and an eddy there, muscle upstream when you have to (and sooner or later, you will have to), or pop into an eddy downstream of a big rock and catch a breather. It's challenging at times, but folks, it's also great fun!

CHAPTER 9

Take-Out: Final Words from Harry

If there's a secret all paddlers share, it's this. All paddling is great paddling, and any watercourse deep enough to float a boat is great paddling water.

So, now you know something about paddling an open canoe with another person, using a style called North American Touring Technique. And I kept the promise I made at the beginning of the book, that I wouldn't use that overwrought phrase again until the last chapter.

This is it. The music ain't goin' round again, so if you want to dance, now's the time. I hope this little book tempts you to dance with your partner in a canoe. I hope it gets you so stoked on paddling that you get off your patio furniture and spend those magical twilight hours on some local waterway every night. I hope it gets you so revved up that you try other kinds of canoeing and other kinds of canoes. They're there: maneuverable little sport tandems, incredibly responsive whitewater boats, big trippers that can swallow a month's worth of gear, and lean, mean racing machines. They're there for solo paddlers, too. It doesn't matter what you like to do; the boats are there to do it.

And I hope you don't neglect kayaks, either. They too come in all sizes and shapes, from long, lean sea tourers to nimble whitewater playboats and those incredible little craft called squirt boats, which are as at home under the water as on the surface. Now that's talking new dimensions in paddling!

And, when you're zipping around on the water somewhere, feeling your muscles working, hearing a good hull carving through the water like the sound of rending silk, sensing and delighting in the skill of your partner, caressing the shaft and the grip of your paddle as you drive into it, let the boat glide for a bit. Let the birds come back to the forest canopy. Watch the slantwise sunlight flicker on the ripples of your passing. Feel your blood moving. Dip up a handful of water and splash it on your face; enjoy the tiny chill it brings. Celebrate sensation. Celebrate living. Celebrate the movement of the boat.

Because it is said that only those who move will die. But paddlers know that those who do not move are already dead.

Index

About the Author and Editor

Author **Harry Roberts**, who died in 1992, was an avid outdoorsman and canoeist who advocated the bent-shaft paddling style, which he labeled the North American Touring Technique. He was editor of *Wilderness Camping* and *Paddler* magazines, founder and editor of *Canoesport Journal*, and marketing head for Hyperform and Sawyer canoes. He is fondly remembered as "Uncle Harry" for his friendly, down-to-earth writing style.

Steve Salins has covered many miles in canoes and kayaks of all types, from whitewater boats to marathon racers. As an instructor for more than twenty years and the "Canoe Technique" columnist for *Canoe & Kayak* magazine, he combines an analytical and direct writing style with an unbridled passion for canoeing.